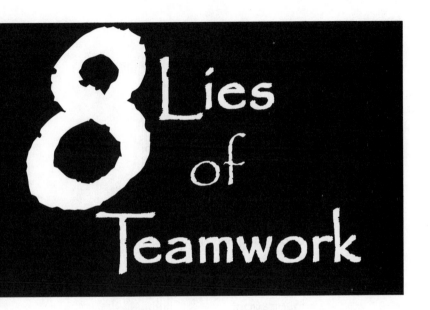

8 Lies of Teamwork

Michael Wachter

This book is dedicated to:

Brett & **Kim**, my son and daughter now pursuing their business careers.

Courtney, my daughter and guardian angel.

Georgann, my wife and inspiration.

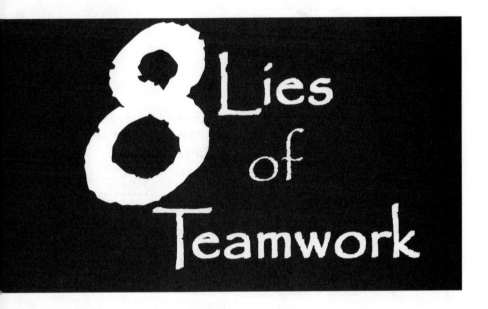

Michael Wachter

ISBN: 0-9661312-3-1
Library of Congress Control Number: 2002105316

Published by **Corporate*Impact***
Avon Lake, Ohio 44012-1230
email: inquiry@CorpImpact.com

Contents

The wonderous wizard brought to the kingdom
a new power called teamwork.

Chapter 1

Introduction

*Why this book, the book's genesis and the
author's credentials (or lack thereof).*

A Fairy Tale

Once upon a time in the Kingdom of Work,
there came a wondrous wizard. The wondrous
wizard brought to the kingdom a new power
called teamwork. When the citizens of the
Kingdom of Work gazed upon it, they mar-
veled at the promise of this new power. And it
was good.

As the wizard spun the teamwork spell, he
strengthened it with other magical new incantations. He added empowerment to
strengthen teamwork by providing greater
decision autonomy. The mighty wizard then
added consensus, a mystical process intended
to make team decisions better than individual

decisions. With the trust incantation, the wondrous wizard begat the dimension of knowing other team members could be counted on to do their part. And then, knowing that supervision was essential to the success of the Kingdom of Work, he summoned the power of a new spell called self-direction. With self-direction, teams could oversee their progress and manage their resources. What could possibly be better than that?

While many of the citizens of the kingdom had aspired to management all their lives, others had already achieved a level of authority in the kingdom. These were called by many names, but all were members of one of three tribes in the kingdom: executives, managers, and supervisors. The wondrous wizard had the ear of the executive tribe, and they sometimes worked to help the incantations succeed. However, the managers tribe and supervisors tribe were another situation all together. These tribes formed a cadre of petty sorcerers to undo the wondrous wizard's powerful spells. You see they had held much power in the Kingdom of Work before the wondrous wizard messed everything up with his teamwork spells. They were not about to give it up.

The petty sorcerers combined all their skills to cast spells that would counter the work of the wondrous wizard. First, they used their most potent weapon, the confusion enchantment. Confusion diffused the power of the wizard's incantations. If no one understood teamwork, empowerment, consensus, trust, and self direction, these would be less of a threat.

They brought the power of their hidden agenda spell to undermine trust. Finally, they added the lip service and withheld resources spells. Lip service allowed the petty sorcerers to look good in the eyes of the executive tribe while withheld resources kept the teamwork spell from having the fuel necessary for its fullest effect. When the citizens of the Kingdom of Work gazed upon hidden agenda, lip service, and withheld resources, they were sore afraid.

Finally, the petty sorcerers combined the power of lip service and confusion to reinvent teamwork. They reasoned that if they could not defeat it, they would transform it into something that they could defeat. This they did with training. Training allowed the petty sorcerers to recast the teamwork spell to their liking. With training, they could redefine teamwork. And, more important – they could lie!

While individually, their powers were weak, there were legions of petty sorcerers. These legions combined their individual strengths and focused them on a common mission. Working as a team, they caused the death of teamwork.

The Real World

OK, maybe it's not a fairy tale. For the past 18 years, I have had the opportunity to work with scores of organizations that had an interest in implementing or improving an existing teamwork program. Over and over I have seen this fairy tale come to life in one form or another.

Perhaps the most obvious example came during a visit to one of Chrysler Corporation's manufacturing facilities. I was working on an assignment for their Executive and Management Education Department and was invited to observe the General Plant Manager's kickoff meeting for Chrysler's new "Corporate Culture Initiative". Under the leadership of former CEO Bob Eaton, Chrysler Corporation had invested many hours of planning in this initiative. The strategy was to use a participative corporate culture as a significant competitive weapon in an industry that is notoriously autocratic. The brand new technology center in Auburn Hills, Michigan was designed to stimulate participation and interaction across Chrysler's many functional groups. Attending the General Plant Manager's kickoff meeting were all of the managers and supervisors in the facility. The corporate staff opened the meeting with a superb, interactive, multimedia presentation on the what, why, and how of the culture change initiative. Then, the General Plant Manager gave an impassioned speech in support of the project. In his speech he strongly supported the concept of teamwork and expounded on the glories of self-directed teams. He challenged his staff to put their best efforts into making the plant a benchmark facility for team-based operations in Chrysler. Then he gave his prediction of success:

> "We're going to have such good teams here that, when we are done, we won't need supervisors anymore, and we'll run this plant with half the present management staff."

Immediately after this pronouncement, a manager seated near me leaned over to one of his peers and said, "This is one initiative I'm going to make sure never gets off the ground."

In one short sentence, the General Plant Manager had effectively cast the "Lip Service" spell and set the initiative up for failure. He tapped into confusion about the role of the supervisor and manager in a team based organization to spread the fear of losing jobs among his entire management staff. This incident, and many like it, stimulated my interest in misconceptions about teamwork and the various devices used by "petty sorcerers" to undermine teamwork.

Incidentally, the General Plant Manager's forecast is a lie. The most effective team based organizations have as many supervisors and managers per capita as do traditional hierarchical organizations. The role changes and becomes more fulfilling, but does not go away. For example, in a traditional hierarchical organization, the supervisor's role is to plan, organize, direct, and control the work of others. In a team-based organization, teams largely perform these functions. The supervisor's role shifts to focus on: lead, teach, build teams, and create a climate for performance (more on this later).

Even in teamwork implementations that have phenomenal success (phenomenal success is excellence on four measures: mission accomplishment, on time, on budget, and team learning), we see petty sorcerers plying their trade. In the mid-1990's Moen Incorporated, established a "Rapid Action Team" (RAT Pack) to respond to customer demands for new product. The team was made up of members from each functional area needed to drive a product to market: engineering, procurement, sales, distribution, and marketing. In one and one half years of operation this team brought more new products to market than the organization had generated in the previous five years combined. Their success earned them the President's Achievement Award for two years in a row. It also earned the envy of many people who were not on the team. The RAT Pack was accused of functioning outside the system, draining resources from other projects, and of being a bunch of braying prima donnas. When Moen hired a new Vice President of Marketing, these petty sorcerers cast the "hidden agenda" spell to influence the new VP to disband the team. Fortunately, Bruce Carbonari, Moen's CEO, was vigilant. He drove a fundamental change in how Moen brought products to market. He directed (yes directed) the new VP of Marketing to structure all product development teams along the lines of the RAT Pack. Cross-functional teams were focused on a broad range of product development activities and RAT Pack members were the primary mentors to these teams. In the following years Moen was able to bring a continuous stream of new and innovative products to market, making the company the number one faucet brand in North America. The errant VP of Marketing has since left the company to pursue other interests.

In all my experience with teams, one core learning stands out from all the others. The harder you push, the harder the organization pushes back. The resistance to effective teamwork is so pervasive in business that only constant vigilance can overcome it. And vigilance requires an understanding of the tools used by petty sorcerers. And that, my friend, is the purpose of this book. I'm going to expose you to the incantations of the petty sorcerers and lay them bare. I'll teach you the lies they use to redefine teamwork so that you will know them when you hear them. And, I'll provide you with a teamwork foundation you can use to set teams free to overachieve in your business.

Who am I to do this? No one special. I'm just a lowly consultant who has worked with many fortune 500 companies and scores of organizations not yet of that size. A minor wizard if you will. One who has studied the ways of the wondrous wizard and the ways of the petty sorcerers. I've met personally with over 100 CEOs and managers to gain insights to their wizardry and their sorcery. I'll bring you my perspectives and share stories of success and failure. Please challenge them and learn from them.

I spent my early career thinking that one day I would have it all figured out. I read and studied everything I could on the topic of management. I knew that I could emerge from the "fog of war" surrounding business to find the panacea of perfection. As I was introduced to more and more companies during my consulting career I did finally figure it out. There will always be problems! The role of a manager and of a consultant is to identify problems and root them out; to wrestle with each one until it is resolved and to put processes in place to prevent its recurrence.

As a member of the executive, management, or supervisor tribe, part of your role is to see these problems through, to see the opportunity that lies inside each problem and to learn from them. This role becomes somewhat easier if you follow in the path of Woodrow Wilson, twenty-eighth President of the United States, who said, "I not only use all the brains I have, but all I can borrow." This is the essence of teamwork. Teams bring the power of multiple minds to bare on solving a common problem. They also provide a vehicle for organizational learning and knowledge transfer, thereby reducing the likelihood of encountering the same problem or problems over and over again.

Be warned! While the process and structure that makes teams work is really quite simple, like any endeavor worth pursuing it will always have problems. Teamwork requires collaborative behaviors and one need only read the early works of naturalists like Desmond Morris, *The Naked Ape* or Robert Ardrey, *The Territorial Imperative* to gain a sense for the competitive nature of the human animal.

One of my associates in Canada points out that, unlike an army of ants or a troop of baboons, we are more like northern timberwolves in our territorial behavior. When a dominant timberwolf loses the battle for supremacy to a stronger opponent, he may choose to form a new pack in a new territory. When he has found a new territory, he carefully marks its boundaries by leaving his scent around the perimeter. I've always found it fascinating to see how many humans engage in symbolically similar behavior surrounding their personal power and corporate position.

The good news is that well structured teams are better equipped to handle problems as they arise. Unlike other organization structures, problem solving and decision making are core competencies resting at the heart of teamwork.

"The problem is not that there are problems.
The problem is expecting otherwise and
thinking that having problems is a problem."

~ Theodore Isaac Rubin, psychiatrist & author

The petty sorcerers say ...

> *Teamwork is separate from the business.*
>
> *Leadership is shared.*
>
> *The team has primary responsibility for team success.*
>
> *There is no "I" in team.*
>
> *Team based organizations use consensus decision making.*
>
> *Teamwork is about relationships.*
>
> *Teamwork requires more meetings.*
>
> *Teams do work.*

Chapter 2

The eight lies

*A summary of the eight lies of teamwork and
the truths that set teams free.*

A Fairy Tale

... and in the Kingdom of Work there is a
hallowed hall. On the walls of the hallowed
hall are written hallowed words. These hallowed words have been amongst us for time
immemorial and will be amongst us for all time
to come. The most hallowed of these hallowed words are parables about teamwork. It
is written that, Teamwork is separate from the
business ... Leadership is shared ... The team
has primary responsibility for team success ...
There is no "I" in team ... Team based organizations use consensus decision making ...
Teamwork is about relationships ... Teamwork requires more meetings ... Teams do

work. And these hallowed writings are lies, all lies!

The Real World

In the evolution of teamwork, consultants and executives have advocated a number of popular myths, misconceptions, and poor practices. Among these myths, misconceptions, and poor practices are what I term "The Eight Lies of Teamwork". In this chapter I'll briefly introduce each of the eight lies and, for each lie, provide a corresponding truth.

The choice for your organization boils down to a reality about teamwork implementations. When teamwork is built on the lies, teamwork fails. When teamwork is based on the truths, teamwork is a powerful tool for success.

The first three lies deal with the role of the executive in relationship to teams.

Lie # 1: Teamwork is separate from the business.

All too often, we encounter teamwork implementations where the impetus for teamwork is an executive's desire to gain cooperation and buy-in from employees or to improve morale. This leads to team training for the masses while the executives continue to conduct business as usual. Business as usual means real decisions are made by the executive and managers deal with problems real to the business. Teams get to make recommendations on unimportant decisions and solve inconsequential problems. This "I'm OK, they're not" mind set creates teamwork separate from the business.

One of our client's had invested heavily with a major consulting firm to set up Employee Involvement Teams (EITs). Regrettably, these teams were structured to practice the "teamwork is separate from the business" approach to teamwork. Employee groups would take time away from their "real job" to work on a decision or problem of the team's choosing. When a team identified an issue important to the business the team was discouraged from pursuing it by being advised, "Management is already working on that." Typical of an EIT problem was the team that took a year to develop an employee cookbook. The cookbook's claim to fame was that the company president had two recipes in the cookbook (he doesn't even cook). Teams got to work on less important decisions and, a manager often overruled even the most insignificant decisions by a team. One EIT met for an hour a week for six weeks to decide what color ashtrays should be used in the break room. They decided on blue. The plant manager disagreed and purchased red ashtrays.

This approach to teamwork required an EIT facilitator at each location, annual employee involvement conferences, a corporate employee involvement manager, and hundreds of indirect labor hours. The net return on this investment was a work force unhappy about not being permitted to participate in the business.

Oh Mama, tell me it isn't so! Based on our experience in many organizations, this experience is not unusual. In fact, it is prevalent in the U.S. automotive industry, and is funded in UAW agreements. It doesn't need to be this way. The solution for our client was to recognize the failure of teamwork separate from the business and begin to practice a new truth about teamwork.

Truth: Teamwork is the way we do business!

Our client defined a new standard for teams in the organization. For a team to exist, it must meet three criteria:

1. Be focused on accomplishment, not activity.

2. Have a clearly defined mission aligned with the strategy of the organization.

3. Have an executive sponsor committed to the team's success.

These three criteria must be met by cross-functional teams and by functional teams.

Cross-functional project teams tackle tactical and strategic problems important to the business. Faced recently with a change in governmental standards that could conceivably have put them out of business our client used *"teamwork as the way we do business."* Six cross-functional teams tackled different aspects of the new regulations and successfully brought the product line into full compliance with the new standards in four months.

In functional areas, the focus on accomplishment and mission definition provided a vehicle to rethink the organization and make it more effective. As a result, the business moved away from a traditional functional structure and organized multi-discipline teams to support the three primary pillars of the company's strategy: high quality customer relationships, superior operations, and best in class speed to market.

Lie #2: Leadership is shared.

The concept of shared leadership in teams confuses the role of the leader with the role of the manager. To best understand this teamwork lie, let us differentiate between *supervise, manage,* and *lead.* When we supervise, we work with people and have the responsibility to develop people capable of excelling in the organization. When we manage we work with projects, things, and processes and have the responsibility to develop projects, things, and processes that permit the organization to excel. When we lead, we define the future of the organization and establish a culture that permits the organization to achieve its potential.

Teams can and do share management responsibility. Self-directed work teams exhibit advanced forms of shared management. However, the responsibility for leadership rests firmly on the shoulders of the executive team.

One of our client organization's teams struggled with a lack of leadership under the "leadership is shared" lie. Cross-functional teams suffered greatly from shared leadership. With shared leadership, teams would charge off in one direction (that advocated by a marketing function leader) only to be pointed in another direction (that advocated by a research development and engineering function leader) the next week. The solution in our client's organization came with the recognition that shared leadership meant no leadership! They began to practice a new truth.

Truth: Management is shared, leadership is the responsibility of the executive team.

Our client's executive team redefined its role in the organization. They stepped away from managing the business and stepped up to leading the business. The executive team decided that:

> The mission of the executive team is to create the vision, develop strategic direction, prioritize key actions, provide resources, and build and lead a participative culture.

Teams with shared management are an integral part of a participative culture. They can supervise and manage. However, the organization's culture is driven purely by the beliefs and behaviors of the organization's appointed leadership, the executive team.

Lie #3: The team has primary responsibility for team success.

This is probably the most insidious of the lies about teamwork. Giving the team primary responsibility for success establishes the team as the scapegoat when teamwork comes up short.

One of the greatest difficulties organizations face in trying to implement a teamwork concept is resistance from management. As noted above, teams can and do exercise supervisory and management authority. As a result, managers tend to see teams as a threat to their position and power. It is at this point that we see the emergence of the "petty sorcerer". A strong functional manager will cause a team to fail by withholding resources and support. Lip service will be paid while passive and active efforts to subvert team success continue. Once these efforts succeed in undermining the team, the guilty manager points an accusing finger at the team concept and casts the petty sorcerers "told you so" spell ... "I told you this wouldn't work. You're trying to turn the asylum over to the inmates!"

This has been a recurring problem as we move away from functional responsibility and authority toward team based action. The solution is taking two paths. One path is a greater emphasis on cross-functional project teams and project management tools. The second path is a new truth.

Truth: The executive sponsor has prime responsibility for team success.

No team should be formed without an executive sponsor committed to its success. The sponsor's role is to empower the team by providing: enablement, definition of scope, freedom to perform, and advocacy. Chapter 5 defines these terms in more detail. For now, it is important to recognize that only after the executive sponsor has fulfilled his or her empowerment role can the team be legitimately held accountable for its success or failure.

The role of the executive.

The first three truths establish the role of the executive in a team-based organization. These are:
- Teamwork must be the way we do business;
- Management is shared, leadership is the responsibility of the executive team; and
- The executive sponsor is responsible for team success.

No executive can be divorced from responsibility for moving the organization forward, providing leadership, or accountability for success/failure. If teamwork is to be successful, the executive must accept it as the vehicle by which the organization obtains results.

Lie #4 There is no "I" in team.

This nasty little lie has been spread in all too many training programs for teams. Even in client organizations where the first three truths were in place, we have seen teamwork struggling because the organization believed that there was no "I" in team. The unfortunate result of accepting this lie is that it permits individuals to abdicate responsibility and avoid accountability. Almost every time we meet with a team for the first time we ask three questions:

> How many of you want to be a member of team where your individual contribution does not count?

> How many of you want to be a member of team where you are not recognized and rewarded for your individual contribution?

> How many of you want to be a member of team where incompetent individuals can hide their incompetence?

The universal answer to these questions is, "**I don't!**" When these conditions exist, competent and dedicated individuals choose not to support teamwork. Organizations that believe there is no "I" in team create an environment where all of these conditions exist. If we want our best performers to role model teamwork in the organization, there must be something in it for them to do so. We must rediscover an old truth.

Truth: Teams are "I"ndividuals focused on a common goal.

The best of teams are made up of powerful individual contributors contributing their best, coordinated, individual efforts to a common goal. Classical team building begins with mission (why do we exist), goals (what will we accomplish), and roles. Role lets the individual team member know what is expected of them. What is expected of every team member is his or her very best effort toward the common goal. In return for that each team member should expect to be recognized and rewarded for his or her efforts.

When the team is made up of significant contributors, each team member is challenged to excel and experiences critical personal rewards by working with others who excel and challenge one another to perform.

Lie #5: Team based organizations use consensus decision making.

For many employees, their first exposure to teamwork in the workplace is some form of consensus decision making exercise. They are stranded on the moon, lost at sea, on a desert island, etc. and left with fifteen to twenty items they must prioritize for survival. At the end of the exercise, the trainer points out how much more effective consensus decision making is and announces that this will become the norm in the organization. Your involvement, and participation in the decision making process of the organization is wanted and welcome. The employee leaves with the common misconception that consensus leadership requires that all decisions, no matter the magnitude, must be made by team consensus. Immediately after this introduction, the employee comes face to face with a decision that was made without that employees input. The reaction is predictable, "They lied to me again!" If we want employee involvement, we must be sure all employees understand the truth about decision making.

Truth: Teams use consensus techniques to make four types of decisions.

In the most advanced of team cultures, decisions are made in many ways. Sometimes the boss makes a nonnegotiable decision without team input. On other occasions the boss gathers team input and then makes an informed decision. Occasionally, the team makes the decision with the boss participating as an equal member. At other times, the team makes the decision and takes action without involving the boss. Consensus is a state of mutual agreement addressing all legitimate concerns of group members that permits all to support the decision. We find consensus techniques, the process of exchanging points of view and listening for understanding, to be useful in all types of decision making. While in reality consensus techniques are used to achieve many decisions of the majority, consensus itself is a hypothetical myth.

Even if true consensus were achieved, every member of the organization would not participate. In one of our large automotive clients, a team of twenty-seven people in a plant of 5,000 employees gathered input from the organization and shared points of view to achieve a "consensus" on an employee recognition program. When their decision was presented to the plant, it was a decision already made and therefore perceived to be an autocratic decision.

Lie #6: Teamwork is about relationships.

Because improved interpersonal relationships help teams be more effective, a great deal of team training has worked on relationships. As a result, many people have the misconception that teamwork is about maintaining good relationships. Consequently, teams will often sacrifice results in order to maintain harmonious relationships.

In one client location members of the executive team were exceedingly polite to one another during team meetings. On leaving the meeting, each would complain about what the others were, or were not, doing. This failure to confront issues in the team led to significant infighting on the team. Among the organization's employees, the executive team was perceived as highly political, not having the interests of the business at heart, and lacking the ability to lead.

When we explored this issue with the team, we learned that their guiding philosophy about teamwork was:

> "You have to play nicely in the sand box. It is not ok to bring up any issue that might offend someone."

The group had placed relationships ahead of results. Thus, they failed to achieve results and they had appalling relationships. Once again, if teamwork is to work, team members must understand the truth.

Truth: Teamwork is about results.

The only reason for using teamwork in an organization is to achieve results. Effective teams focus on achieving results and work toward relationships that support accomplishment. The only reason for teams to maintain relationships is because groups working in harmony tend to achieve the best results.

Rest assured, if teamwork does not generate results for an organization, the organization will bring in an autocratic manager to get things done. Given a choice between achieving results and getting along, an organization will choose results every time!

Lie #7: Teamwork requires more meetings.

The most common complaint we hear about teamwork is that it ties people up in meetings. It is true that it is very difficult to work as a team if the team never meets. However, our experience is that teamwork can have the effect of reducing the number of meetings people attend.

Many of our client organizations consume innumerable hours in meetings; meetings to communicate, meetings about problems, meetings to plan, meetings to organize, meetings, meetings, meetings. The reality is organizations are awash with meetings and most of them do not accomplish much. There is a little secret not often understood about teamwork - for teamwork to work, teamwork must make your meetings more effective. That is one of our truths.

Truth: Teamwork makes meetings more effective .

One of the hidden powers of teamwork is the ability to focus meetings on accomplishing results rather than activities. Teams meet to plan, organize, problem solve, and make decisions. When an effective team meets, it generates results. In doing so, the team addresses many of the issues on which the organization was already consuming meeting time. Effective meetings are essential to effective teamwork. Otherwise, teamwork does require more meetings and, in so doing, does not work. Teams drive effective meetings with five guiding principles:

1. A meeting may not be held unless the purpose is clearly stated.

2. The outcomes the meeting must achieve are defined before the meeting starts.

3. Participation is predicated on the individual's ability to contribute to the meeting or the meeting's ability to contribute to the individual.

4. Ground rules encourage every participant to "cause a good meeting."

5. The meeting closes with a review of what was, or was not **accomplished**!

Lie # 8: Teams do work.

Without doubt, our most interesting discovery is this last lie. The name itself, teamwork, implies that teams do work. Earlier in this chapter, we stated a truth; teamwork is about results. This truth would seem to imply that teams do work. However, in all of our client organizations, we have discovered there is a limited set of activities a team actually undertakes as a team. And, the vast majority of these activities are the work of thinking as opposed to the work of doing. When it comes to actually doing something, another earlier truth comes to play; teams are individuals focused on a common goal. To actually do something, some individual team member has to do it. This leads to our last truth.

Truth: Teams think, team members do work.

The things teams do well include many thinking activities: When teams are effective, they:

- Analyze situations
- Problem solve
- Plan
- Brain storm
- Coordinate
- Make decisions
- Exchange information
- Follow-up/review progress

All of these activities are thinking processes necessary for generating results. However to begin implementation of a plan or decision, individual team members must do work.

The truths set teams free.

Through these eight lies and countless other incantations, the petty sorcerers amongst us often manage to derail the best efforts of a truly participative leader to establish a foundation of teamwork in the organization. We will explore each of these in greater depth in the succeeding chapters. And, we will examine the basic process for establishing team-based activity in your organization. As we proceed, you'll learn how to implement the truths that set teams free.

"He who is unable to live in society, or who has no need because he is sufficient for himself, must be either a beast or a god."

~ Aristotle (384BC - 322BC) Greek writer, philosopher

"Perhaps," says the petty sorcerer, "we can give teams something safe to do. You know, something away from the business!"

The wonderous wizard thinks, "this would be a terrible waste of resources, teamwork must be the way we do business!"

Chapter 3:

Teamwork is separate from the business

The quality circle game.

A Fairy Tale

"That foolish wizard intends to let the people
of the kingdom hold the reins of power in their
hands," fretted the petty sorcerer. "There
must be a way to avoid this?"

Then the multitude of petty sorcerers gathered to plot plots and plan plans. In the midst
of their plotting and planning they came upon a
form of compromise! "We can give the people
an opportunity to learn teamwork by practicing
it in a 'safe' environment," one said. "We'll give
them a place to play, but be sure they don't
touch anything important. Then they will be
impotent, and in their impotence they will begin
to believe teamwork is impotent."

"What shall we call this plan?" another asked. "We should not call it recess, that would be to obviously the truth." "Quality Circles," someone shouted. "Employee Involvement Teams, "shouted another.

And so it came to pass that ...

The Real World

Whether intentionally or unintentionally, this fairy tale is often set up as reality. Teams, which have no impact on the business, are set up to give employees the impression they are involved, or to provide a learning opportunity, or to satisfy a labor contract requirement. Regardless of the reason, it is teamwork outside the business, a practice that is unproductive, wasteful, and that employees see through instantly.

I recently interviewed a senior manager in one of my automotive clients about their use of "quality circles" and "employee involvement teams". The company defined a quality circle as a shop floor group that met for an hour a week to address issues of quality in their work area. The "circle" selected the matter they wanted to look at and pursued that topic independently. Each "circle" could make recommendations to management but had no authority to implement suggestions without approval. Employee involvement teams were structured the same way with the exception that they were not specifically chartered to work on quality issues. They could select any area they wished and pursue it.

These teams met for an hour once a week to "work on their problem." Once a quarter one, or more of the teams would make a presentation to a management group. The presentation included a definition of the problem and the team's recommendations on what needed to be done to resolve it. When I asked the senior manager how well this approach worked, he looked chagrined and said, "To tell you the truth, what we usually get from the teams is a to-do list for our managers and our managers plates are already full. It's a real catch-22. We want their input, but we don't have the resources to act on it."

The management team was working off a priority analysis of issues in the plants. The issues surfaced by the employee teams tended to be so far down the priority pile that they rarely got action. The business was guilty of practicing the "Teamwork is separate from the business" lie. The company had an established business process to identify issues and prioritize them for action, but the teams were set up outside of this process. Consequently any issues a team addressed that were too low on the priority list got no management action. In addition the teams needed management approval to act. As a result, rather than act on their own recommendations, teams attempted to delegate upward by proposing solutions requiring management action.

If management really wanted employee teams to be effective, they needed to integrate the team activity with the way the company does business.

Another example comes from a massive information technology and business process improvement project at Fortune Brands Home and Office Products Group. Project team members were drawn from all parts of the organization. The teams charter was to define and implement improved business processes and put in place information technology systems to support them. This was a critical strategic initiative for the business and was thoroughly integrated to the business.

However the training aspect of the project was structured differently. Recruited predominantly from outside the business, the training team was not integrated with the project. Rather, they were set up to stand beside the project. Their work area was remote from the project team, but they were expected to gather information from the project team. The trainers' charter was to develop the training materials needed to successfully implement the new processes and systems.

As you might expect, this proved to be a problem area for the project as a whole. The training group was always playing catch-up. They did not get information until the absolute deadline and the resultant learning curve was entirely too steep to climb. The rest of the project team did not see training as part of their charter. They considered the trainers to be bothersome and an impediment to their progress. After suffering through one phase of the project under this structure, the project's management team recognized their mistake. They had set the training team up for failure by creating a team outside the business. Fortunately, this management team knew the truth about teamwork. That is, if we choose to use teamwork, it must be the way we do business.

Truth: Teamwork is the way we do business.

The project was restructured so that trainers were part of the project team. In addition, the process definition and improvement teams were given the goal of implementing effective training on the new processes and systems. Trainers participated in the full endeavor with the rest of the team. As a result, training was not only ahead of the curve, but also the training professionals were considered to be an integral and important part of the project's ultimate success.

If we want to get results from teamwork, we must make teamwork the way we do business. In the first example in this chapter, the automotive example, the firm needed to involve the teams in the issue identification and prioritizing process. This would integrate the teams with the way the company did business. When asked why this was not so, the VP said that the company's objective for the employee teams was to gather some of the "low hanging fruit" (easy issues with easy solutions) that fell beneath management's radar. If that is the case, the way the company said it wanted to do business and the way it did business were not in sync. For teams to gather "low hanging fruit" they must have the resources to do so and be empowered to take action on their own within defined boundaries.

Let's take a look at a more effective approach. In 1979 I worked at the Glidden Paint Plant in Huron, Ohio. Production employee teams were asked to identify and address safety issues in the plant and were authorized to take action within a defined budget as long as the action did not violate an existing safety policy. As such they were focused on issues important to the business, were provided the resources, and were empowered to implement solutions within defined boundaries. Under this initiative employees began a shop floor safety inspection team, safety training, policed their areas, and monitored their coworker's safety practices. This led to an unprecedented two plus years with no lost time or recordable injuries in the plant.

How to make it work.

If your business is going to use teams and teamwork, three simple steps will make teamwork the way we do business.

1. Focus teamwork efforts on issues that are important to the business.

2. Establish executive sponsorship.

3. Empower teams to implement decisions within defined boundaries.

Using these techniques, we get the kind of results demonstrated at Glidden.

Focus teamwork efforts on issues that are important to the business.

One of the fundamental elements of teamwork is mission. Mission tells you why the team exists and what it is expected to achieve. Every organization has cultural, strategic, process, and financial imperatives that define what work gets done. Teamwork is nothing more than a tool to implement culture, strategy, process, and financial imperatives. Efforts to built teamwork outside the context of these organizational drivers are doomed to fail, and they should fail. Why, because they are not designed to support the business imperatives; thus they are an inappropriate use of resources.

You have a process to improve, establish a team of people whose mission is to improve it. You have a strategy to develop, set up a team of people whose mission is to develop it. You have a problem to solve, start a team of people whose mission is to solve it. If you just want to make people feel good, throw a party. It is a lot cheaper than setting up teamwork outside the business. Also, when the team's mission is accomplished, disband the team and shift the individual resources to another issue important to the business. This way, teamwork is self-renewing.

Establish executive sponsorship.

The most productive use of human capital is on a team with a clear organizational mission and strong executive sponsorship. The clear mission focuses the team's efforts on issues important to the business. Executive sponsorship clears the decks for the team to succeed.

The executive sponsor is responsible for providing leadership to the team (we'll look at the "leadership is shared" lie in the next chapter). As part of this leadership the sponsor insures the team understands its mission and the alignment of that mission to the organization's driving imperatives. The sponsorship also insures appropriate resources for success and provides the boundaries for the team's decision authority. Having done so, the sponsor must champion the team and the team's accomplishments in the larger organization. And, perhaps most important of all, when the mission has been accomplished, the sponsor will understand the wisdom of Chinese philosopher Lao Tzu, "Of a good leader the people will say, we did it ourselves."

Empower teams to implement decisions within defined boundaries.

Even in the most autocratic of traditional hierarchical structures, subordinates are given a degree of freedom to act in performance of the assigned job. Teams are no different. They are groups of people giving their best individual effort to a common goal. To best succeed at accomplishing that common goal, teams need a degree of freedom to act without seeking permission. Part of the role of the team sponsor is to define the boundaries within which the team is free to implement decisions and assure the resources required to do so. I'll expand on this concept in chapter 5.

Suffice it to say, to make teamwork the way we do business, we should operate teamwork the way Warren Buffett operates Berkshire Hathaway. In his 1998 Letter to Shareholders, Buffett says:

"At Berkshire we feel that telling outstanding CEOs, such as Tony Nicely (CEO of GEICO), how to run their companies would be the height of foolishness. Most of our managers wouldn't work for us if they got a lot of backseat driving... Nevertheless, Berkshire's ownership may make even the best of managers more effective. First we eliminate all of the ritualistic and nonproductive activities that normally go with the job of CEO. Our managers are totally in charge of their personal schedules. Second, we give each a simple mission: Just run your business as if: 1) you own 100% of it; 2) it is the only asset in the world that you and your family have or will ever have; and 3) you can't sell or merge it for at least a century. As a corollary, we tell them they should not let any of their decisions be affected even slightly by accounting considerations. We want our managers to think about what counts, not how it will be counted."

Replace the term CEO with the term TEAM and you have it!

"We have always found that people are most productive in small teams with tight budgets, time lines and the freedom to solve their own problems."

~ John Rollwagen, chairman and chief executive officer of Cray Research, Inc.

"If teamwork is so great, let leadership be shared."

"It would be a mistake to confuse leadership with management or supervision. Teams can, and do, share management responsibilities, but leadership is the responsibility of the executive team.

Chapter 4

Leadership is shared

The lie that sets teams up to fail.

A Fairy Tale

Not satisfied with inventing teamwork outside
the business, the petty sorcerers in the Kingdom of Work continued their plotting and
planning. Among their more significant subterfuges was a bit of confusion about self-
direction. After all, the wonderful wizard
himself had cast an incantation permitting
teams to be self-directed, and the prophecies
foretold that a leader would walk among us in
our time of need.

How simple it was for the petty sorcerers to
recast the spell to "leadership is shared."
"You'll see," said the sorcerer, "with shared
leadership, there will be no leadership at all

and the people will cry out for the blood of the executive tribe."

And, in the fullness of time, the kingdom was beset by lack of direction and inconsistency. "Where are our leaders?" the people wondered. " Why have they abandoned us?"

The Real World

A great deal has been written in the past decade advocating self-directed work teams. However, it is important to note that self-directed does not mean self-led. Teams supervise. They plan, organize, assign work to team members, follow-up on assignments, and control performance. Teams also manage. They implement work processes, seek continuous improvement, and oversee the assets allocated to them. The reality is that the inherent ability of teams to supervise and manage is threatening to the traditional manager and supervisor, thus it gives rise to the petty sorcerer. Nevertheless the fact that teams exercise significant management and supervisory responsibility does not equate to leadership being shared.

In *Inspirational Quotes & Insights for Leaders*, Warren G. Bennis says, "Failing organizations are usually over-managed and under-led." We agree that there is a significant difference between leadership and management. Although self-directed teams exercise significant self-management and self-supervision, it is the role of the leader to establish the vision and mission that drives team action.

One of my clients is a large private design firm. The President and CEO of the firm exercises a highly participative form of leadership and encourages a free wheeling, innovative culture. In his early efforts at teamwork and participation, he attempted to have his senior staff team come to consensus on fundamental leadership decisions. In doing this he discovered that the staff would circle an issue for hours at a time, never coming to a decision. When he endeavored to drive the team to closure on an issue, conflicting points of view would prevent a decision being made. It didn't take long for him to learn that he needed to make the decision himself if one was going to get made. To keep with his participative leadership style, he now solicits input from his senior staff team and encourages a free wheeling discussion. He then makes his own decision.

This behavior is consistent with what we see from the more notable corporate leaders, both past and present. Be it Jack Welch at GE, Jack Breen at Sherwin Williams, Lee Iacocca or Bob Eaton at Chrysler, Gene Winfeld at Kirby, Bruce Carbonari at Fortune Brands, or any of a host of others. They do not lead by committee, and they do not delegate their leadership prerogative to a team. However, virtually all believe in and practice teamwork as the way to get business results.

It requires a leader to identify and charter the team. Leaders instill vision, meaning, and trust. They empower followers. Leaders also exercise power, the ability to translate intention into reality, by initiating and sustaining action. Teamwork is essentially a vehicle for translating intention into reality. It is one of the tools of leadership!

When we attempt to delegate leadership to teams, we set up "bid for power" dynamics. Bid for power occurs when individuals seek to exercise power and authority over other team members or other teams. Without clear leadership (or with shared leadership), this becomes a perpetual state, degenerating from an attempt at teamwork to something far more akin to medieval tribal warfare.

The DaimlerChrysler "merger" provides a top level case in point. The joining of these two organizations was characterized as a merger of equals. Even leadership roles were to be shared by Daimler executives and Chrysler executives. Once shareholders had approved the "merger," it did not take long for two truths to shine the light of reality on Daimler's acquisition of Chrysler Corporation. The first of these truths was that the former Daimler Corporation held the majority interest in the new DaimlerChrysler. The second truth was the cultures of the two organizations were radically different.

By automotive standards, Chrysler was innovative, flexible, and practiced participatory decision making throughout most of the organization. They also had a reputation for inferior quality. Daimler had a reputation for superior quality but was slow to act, rigid, and practiced top down decision making throughout most of the organization. They also showed great deference to hierarchical status. As these two cultures clashed, the new organization was pulled in many directions. Conflict developed between leaders from the Chrysler culture and leaders from the Daimler culture. In the midst of the ongoing bid for power, no unifying strategic direction was apparent and DaimlerChrysler's performance measures plummeted.

The need for clear, consistent leadership led to the end of the shared executive leadership experiment as former Daimler CEO Jurgen Schrempp assumed control and, beginning with former Chrysler CEO Bob Eaton, Chrysler executives left the business in droves. The company and its employees learned a very painful lesson, shared leadership means no leadership at all.

The confusion arises when we fail to differentiate between lead, supervise, and manage. All to often we hear the three terms used interchangeably. While they do have some overlap, they are not the same.

Truth: Management is shared – leadership is the responsibility of the executive team.

In its purest form, the role of the leader is to provide a clear vision of the future, succinct direction for the present, and a consistent culture for performance. Given clarity from the organization's leadership, teams implement these elements and team members share responsibility for focusing on them.

The traditional definition of supervise is: plan, organize, and control the work of others. In a team based organization, the team does the planning, organizing, and controlling. This reality leads to the misconception that leadership is shared. Teams are fully capable of supervising their own activity and team members do share responsibility to plan, organize, and control the work of the team. However the role of supervisor does not go away, instead it changes. The new role is built around the continuing need for every member of the organization to build new skills and gain new knowledge. The supervisor in a team based organization coaches, teaches, builds teams, and creates a climate for performance. In so doing, the supervisor develops people capable of excelling in a team based organization.

The manager's role typically involves making tactical decisions, husbanding resources, defining processes, and enforcing process discipline. Once again, in a team based organization, the team makes tactical decisions, husbands resources, defines processes, and enforces process discipline. But the role of manager does not go away. A manager must still allocate resources across several teams, form teams around tactical and strategic business requirements, ensure consistent business process across team and functional boundaries, and share process improvements across the organization.

In short, self-directed teams are self-managed and self-supervised. They receive leadership from the executive team and support from supervisory and management staff.

How to make it work.

If your organization seeks to have self-managed teams, there are three fundamentals that must be in place:

1. Teams are structured to accomplish the initiatives and goals established by the strategic plan.

2. Reward systems are designed to support strategic success.

3. Teamwork is viewed as a critical process in the organization, requiring continuous process improvement and process discipline.

4. The supervisor's role is reoriented to coaching, teaching, building teams, and creating a climate for performance.

Teams are structured to accomplish the initiatives and goals established by leadership's strategic plan.

When teams become the vehicle for implementing strategic initiatives, we begin to see the true power of teamwork in an organization. Perhaps the best way to visualize this relationship is by looking at the structure of a good strategic plan with linkage from top to bottom. Leadership establishes the plan to provide direction and focus. Management implements the plan by building teams to accomplish elements of the plan. Teams form the organization units through which work gets done.

The strategic plan begins with a clear vision of the future defining what the organization is in the process of becoming. Vision establishes direction and is the province of leadership. Flowing from the vision is a mission statement that focuses on the present and says what the organization is about today. The vision and mission are pursued in a desired culture that defines the shared values by which the business is conducted. Mission and culture definition are also the province of leadership.

Initiatives and goals define specifically what needs to be accomplished. Processes define the methodologies used to drive initiative and goal fulfillment. And finally all of this is accomplished via an organization structure designed to fulfill the initiatives. Team based organizations use teams as part of the organization structure. They build teams around strategic initiatives and strategic goals.

49

STRATEGIC PLAN

Vision	What we are in the process of becoming or achieving in the future.	Established by leadership
Mission	What we are focused on today.	Established by leadership
Culture	The values and behaviors by which we conduct our business.	Established by leadership
Initiatives	Primary drivers to achieve the vision, mission, and culture.	Established by leadership
		Refined by management
		Pursued by teams
Goals	Time referenced deliverables for each initiative.	Established by management
		Reviewed by leadership
		Pursued by teams
Processes	Work methods to facilitate goal accomplishment.	Established by management or teams
		Refined by teams
Structure	Organization design that best pursues the strategy.	Drives team formation

Reward systems are designed to support strategic success.

The old adage, "that which gets rewarded gets done," still holds true. Yet, I never cease to be amazed at the frequency with which reward systems discourage supporting the company's strategy. The business strategy defines the common goals of the organization and reward systems must be designed to encourage people to pursue those goals. Only when people and reward systems are structured around strategic goals has leadership created organizational alignment to the strategy.

For example, when Lee Iacocca first assumed control of Chrysler Corporation, the company had a huge inventory of unsold cars and was continuing to add vehicles to that inventory. Iacocca demanded that the manufacturing facilities scale back production and begin to build only vehicles for which there was a dealer order. Chrysler plant managers' bonus compensation was based on the number of vehicles they produced. As a result, they kept building vehicles! Plant managers' behavior did not support the stated goals of the organization until the reward structure was changed.

By structuring teams around strategic initiatives we align human resources in support of strategic goals. But if the reward structure is in conflict, the goal is not in common. Individuals pursue that which is rewarded rather than that which is in the plan. By aligning reward systems to strategic initiatives, we eliminate the all too frequent conflict between goals and rewards. We also eliminate one of the common causes of conflict in teams.

Teamwork is viewed as a critical process in the organization, requiring continuous process improvement and process discipline.

One critical role of managers in any organization is to ensure consistent performance through repeatable processes. Management puts great effort into defining, refining, and implementing the processes by which the company develops products, gets orders, fulfills orders, and gets paid for the order. In a team based organization, teamwork is the foundation process by which all these activities get done. As such management must invest substantial effort in defining, refining, and implementing the teamwork process.

The supervisor's role is reoriented to coaching, teaching, building teams, and creating a climate for performance.

The greatest threat to effective teamwork is a supervisor who perceives that s/he no longer has a role in the organization. As stated before, the traditional supervisory functions are conducted rather well by teams. However, the organization still requires people who "get work done through others". But the role must move from cop to coach, from disciplinarian to teacher, from boss to team builder. Most important, the supervisor insures a climate for performance by assuring that each team has mission and role clarity.

"Give to us clear vision that we may know where to stand and what to stand for—because unless we stand for something, we shall fall for anything."

~ Peter Marshall (1902 - 1949) US religious leader Prayer at Senate opening 1947.

"We must give the team primary responsibility for team success."

"The team certainly must accept responsibility for success. However the executive sponsor has the **primary** responsibility.

Chapter 5

The team has primary responsibility for team success

The lie used to destroy teamwork.

A Fairy Tale

As the power of the wonderful wizard's team-work spells bore fruit, the forces of good slowly began to overwhelm the forces of evil. Teams were formed throughout the kingdom and all manner of undertakings were under-taken. However, in a dark corner of the kingdom was a dark cave. And in that dark cave was a great power, the power of account-ability. Petty sorcerers had hidden account-ability away in this darkest of caves in the darkest of corners in order to keep it from interfering with their pitiful little empires.

"Perhaps it is time to let accountability out of the cave," whispered a simple sorcerer. "We can hold teams accountable for their success. Then we can cause them to fail. After all, the executive tribe loves accountability. They will think us wonderful for bringing it to bear on the powers of teamwork. We can hold teams accountable and avoid any accountability for ourselves."

And so, it came to pass that the petty sorcerers would hold teams accountable for success while, at the same time, taking actions designed to undermine that very success.

The Real World

So you think the story above is a fairy tale do you. I must admit that I am a firm believer in accountability. However, accountability begins at the top of the organization and works its way down. Leadership must always have prime accountability for success or failure. If not, we empower leaders and managers to cause teams to fail. Just in case you disagree, let me share a story.

In March of 2000, the senior management of a machine tool company outside of Chicago established a team of middle managers and supervisors to implement lean manufacturing techniques and reduce the order to delivery time in their manufacturing operations. Because this fell in the scope of responsibility held by the Executive Vice President of Operations, he was considered the team's sponsor. Unfortunately, this EVP was the ultimate petty sorcerer. He firmly believed that he knew everything there was to know about machine tool manufacturing and everything there ever would be. He had personally designed the existing manufacturing plan and shop floor layout and his ego would not permit him to accept the possibility that a team of "junior" people could improve it.

In meetings with other executive staff members the EVP paid extensive lip service to the project and its goals. Outside these meetings, he did everything in his power to cause the effort to fail. He piled additional project assignments on the team members, prevented people from attending team meetings, and overruled the most basic of lean manufacturing suggestions. While all of this was going on, the EVP was reworking the manufacturing plan and shop floor layout on his own.

As the team struggled against the barriers placed before it by the EVP, he was "holding the team accountable" for their lack of success in senior staff meetings. He railed about their poor performance and criticized the entire concept of putting a team of "junior" people in charge of such an important project. The EVP actively campaigned to have the team disbanded. By the end of the year, the team was in total disarray. Further, the senior staff was so embroiled in power politics that the effort was beyond salvage.

The team and its members were held accountable for the teams failure and, at this writing, most of the team members have left the company. I think it is very clear who is accountable for the failure of this team and it is not the team or the team members! That's the problem with accountability. The team should have it, but the executive sponsor has to have it too.

Unfortunately, this story is a long way from being an isolated incident. One of the greatest difficulties organizations face when implementing a team concept is resistance from management. The source of this resistance is broad and insidious. Sometimes a manager fears his or her job will be eliminated. Other managers fear losing authority or prestige. Still others are on a massive power or ego trip. Regardless of the source, managers who want teamwork to fail have many tools at their disposal to cause that failure. As lip service is paid to the team effort, actions are taken to undermine it.

While many of us wish it were not so, empire building and petty politics are often the rule, not the exception, not only in corporate life but also in our social activities. I am an active member of several scuba diving clubs and several years ago I was asked to develop safe diving guidelines for one of the clubs. Being a firm believer in teamwork, I established a team of members to develop the guidelines. We invited any member who wished to participate, and we specifically recruited members who were scuba instructors. One instructor, who conducted the club sponsored scuba classes, flat out refused to participate in the process. The team gathered guidelines from other clubs, scuba certifying agencies and dive charter operators. They spent a great deal of time comparing and contrasting these guidelines and then published preliminary safe diving principles for review by the club's membership and trustees. The plan was then modified based on input from the membership and trustees.

As soon as the final guidelines were published, the instructor who had refused to participate sent a letter to the director of the YMCA where the club met and to several certifying agencies alleging that the club was unsafe and not following established scuba safety practices. He demanded that the club be banned from further use of YMCA facilities. He also came to the next club trustee meeting armed with correspondence he had sent, research he had conducted, and a set of guidelines he had developed on his own while the team was doing its work.

Here was a highly qualified individual who had a great deal to offer the team effort. Rather than participate in the process, he chose to attempt to play power politics. Why? Was his ego threatened? Did he feel some loss of power and authority? I don't know. What I do know is that this individual is also a sales manager for one of the largest companies in the United States. Now I ask you, how do you think he acts in the workplace?

Because people like this exist and hold positions of power and authority in the workplace, it is important to understand the basic truth about accountability for team success.

Truth: The executive sponsor has prime responsibility for team success.

In the early stages of implementing a team concept at one of my client companies we were encountering significant resistance from several senior managers, including the Vice President Operations. He once told me, "I'm from the old school. When I say jump, my people are supposed to salute and ask how high." I asked him if he thought he was capable of changing and he answered, "Not if I can help it."

With the help of the CEO, we structured teams so that each had an executive sponsor. The sponsors were advised that they would be held personally accountable for the teams success or failure. It was their job to make the effort work. Further, a significant portion of the sponsors' incentive compensation was tied to the successful accomplishment of team missions. The results were phenomenal. Teams suddenly had access to the resources and skills needed to succeed. They had a clear understanding of what was expected of them, the mission, the objectives, the outcomes to be accomplished and what was outside the scope of the team. Sponsors became advocates for their teams. They actively worked to remove roadblocks and gave the teams the freedom to succeed.

In a follow-up meeting with the Vice President Operations I was seeking his input and feedback on the process. His first piece of feedback was that I was a son of a bitch! When I asked him to explain he said, "I told you I was from the old school and didn't intend to change. As it turned out, I had no option. Not only are you a son of a bitch, you're a conniving son of a bitch. And I'm glad you are." This crusty old warrior from the old school had seen the light. Not because he wanted to, but because he had to. He became one of the strongest advocates of teamwork I have ever known.

The lesson is, no team should be formed without an executive sponsor committed to its success. The sponsor's role is to empower the team by providing enablement, definition, freedom, and advocacy. These elements, defined below, are fundamental to the leader's role and essential to team success.

The empowerment elements are defined as follows:

1. **Enablement**: access to the knowledge, resources, and skills needed to succeed.

2. **Definition**: a clear understanding of the mission, objectives, and outcomes the team must achieve and the limits of the team's scope (what they are not expected to achieve).

3. **Freedom**: the freedom to operate within the boundaries established in the mission and scope.

4. **Advocacy**: providing the clout to insure the organization does not prevent the team's success.

Should any of these four elements of sponsorship be absent, a team failure is primarily the responsibility of the sponsor, not the team. Only after these four elements are in place can the team to be legitimately held accountable for its success or failure.

How to make it work.

Three basic elements are necessary to insure sponsorship:

1. Assign a management/executive sponsor to every team.

2. Hold the sponsor accountable for the success of the team.

3. Hold team kick off and team progress sessions with the sponsor.

Assign a management/executive sponsor to every team.

In all traditional organizational structures, executive/management sponsorship is provided to each organizational unit in the structure. The typical functional organization has a Vice President and one or more directors who sponsor activity in departmental units. The matrix organization attempts to break down functional boundaries by providing multiple sponsors to each operational unit. Teams are simply another organizational unit. As with any other organization unit, teams require executive/management sponsors to provide leadership and remove obstacles to success. No team, functional or cross-functional, should ever be formed without first identifying the appropriate leadership sponsor.

Hold the sponsor accountable for the success of the team.

Just as you should hold management accountable for success in a functional organization, team sponsors are accountable for team success. This includes believing in the old management axiom, "That which gets paid for gets done!" Make the performance of the teams under a manager's sponsorship part of that manager's compensation.

The sponsor provides access to the knowledge, resources, and skills necessary to achieve the team's mission. S/he provides clarity of direction, mentoring, and barrier removal.

Hold team kick off and team progress sessions with the sponsor.

To start a team well, the sponsor must orchestrate a team kickoff meeting that clarifies the team's mission and goals, the role each team member is expected to fulfill, how the team will get work done, the resources available, any limitations on the team, and what the team can expect from the sponsor.

To keep it on track, the sponsor needs to have periodic progress reviews to revisit and reinforce the team's mission and goals, the role each team member is expected to fulfill, and what the team can expect from the sponsor. These sessions serve to help keep the team focused and to notify the sponsor of any assistance s/he needs to provide.

Once the sponsor has demonstrated fulfillment of the sponsorship role, the team can and should be held accountable for success.

"You can't run a society or cope with its problems if people are not held accountable for what they do."

~ John Leo (1913 - 1993) English biologist, essayist

"There is no "I" in team.

*"There must be 'I's in team.
After all, teamwork is
"I"ndividuals focused on a
common goal."*

Chapter 6

There is no "I" in team

The most obvious lie.

A Fairy Tale

Before the gathered masses stood a petty sorcerer called by the name team trainer. "I bring you great news of teamwork," declared the sorcerer, "There is no I in team." Then the sorcerer wrote on his magical slate these four letters: T E A M. Pointing at each letter he declared, "See, there is no I in this word. Each individual must subordinate his or her self-interest to the team if the team is to succeed."

The Real World

Unfortunately, this fairy tale occurs in almost every training program that provides an introduction to teamwork. The trainer emphasizes that the goals of the team must be held above all others and goes on to say, "there is no I in team, you must subordinate your interests to the goals of the team." The message received is that individual contributors must set their goals and aspirations aside. The reaction of strong individual contributors to this message is absolutely predictable, "**I** don't need to be involved in this." And the best individual contributors choose to opt out of teamwork efforts early on. The reality is that one hand washes the other. Organizational goals are best met by talented individuals giving their best individual effort toward a common goal. Individual contributor's goals and aspirations are best met through successful contributions to a team effort. Let's examine a range of examples.

My wife recently completed a watercolor that shows a commercial "hard hat" diver entering the water off the side of a work boat. Looking at the picture, I began to consider the teamwork depicted in the painting. The diver is the only one entering the water. However, s/he is supported by at least five team members. One person insures the compressor supplying breathing air to the diver is uninterrupted. Another maintains communications with the diver. Yet another tends the umbilical lines from the boat to the diver. A second diver is standing by to provide assistance if needed. And, a medic is prepared to treat any emergency situation. Each of these people is highly skilled and each plays a specific role in accomplishing a common objective. Should any of these individuals fail to fulfill the role they have in this team effort, the effort will fail.

A commercial diver friend, Mike King, recently experienced this truth. He was working in a local harbor removing old dock pilings when, without warning, his air supply stopped. Fortunately, Mike had an emergency air supply (scuba tank) as part of his equipment set up and was able to switch to scuba and come to the surface. Once on the surface he learned the person responsible for operating the air compressor had fallen asleep and allowed the compressor to run out of fuel. That fellow is no longer a member of Mike's team.

The effort clearly requires teamwork, a group of individuals giving their **best efforts** toward a common goal. Each individual has a contribution to make and each individual is able to advance their own career and interests by excelling in the teams objectives. Otherwise, teams become places for incompetent people to hide and the competent folks bail out.

Authors are fond of using sports examples to describe how teamwork works. However, every sports team analogy I have read leaves out a fundamental part of the equation. Players compete for positions on sports teams and only the very best make it. Sports teams weed out the under performers before they ever take the field! Legendary football coach Vince Lombardi once said, *"The achievements of an organization are the results of the combined effort of each individual."* To win a championship, each individual player must not only fulfill the role they have on the team, but excel at it.

For the individual to maximize their personal success, the team must flourish. Focusing the efforts of strong individuals to a common goal is what teamwork is all about. However, if one focuses effort at a common goal and denies the opportunity for each individual to achieve their own personal goals, one sets up the parameters for failure.

In *I Can't Accept Not Trying*, Michael Jordan, one of the greatest basketball players of all time, offers: "There are plenty of teams in every sport that have great players and never win titles. Most of the time, those players aren't willing to sacrifice for the greater good of the team. The funny thing is, in the end, their unwillingness to sacrifice only makes individual goals more difficult to achieve. One thing I believe to the fullest is that if you think and achieve as a team, the individual accolades will take care of themselves. Talent wins games, but teamwork and intelligence win championships." This said, throughout his playing career, whenever the game was on the line, Jordan wanted the ball in his own hands. Why? Because he had supreme confidence in his own ability.

It is the combined effort of each individual, the "**I**" in team, which makes teamwork a powerful tool. When strong individuals work toward common goals, the results advance the individual's interests as well as the team's interests. Just as the organization needs to treat teamwork as the way we do business, individuals need to treat teamwork as the way we each succeed. What team trainers should be advocating is that individual goals and aspirations are most often achieved through teamwork.

One of our clients was recently involved in the planning for an after-prom party for his daughter's high school. He was so impressed by the teamwork demonstrated by the parents that he spent time examining what made the efforts so successful. Clearly, the parents shared a common goal: to provide a safe and memorable after-prom experience for their children. In addition, each parent joined the effort by asking "What can **I** do?" The parents provided their best individual effort to a common goal and each parent achieved personal rewards by being involved in the effort. The synergy between achieving team goals and supporting individual goals is the formula that drives success.

My daughter recently received her undergraduate business degree from Ohio University. The emphasis in this school and in schools across the nation is on team learning. Students work on projects as a group. They study in study groups. And, they give class presentations as a group. There is no formal teamwork training. However, the students quickly learn the formula for success is to capitalize on the strengths each individual brings to the team. They also learn very quickly, which individuals they do not want on the team.

By using this approach, the school has accomplished several objectives. The percentage of students failing to complete the program has declined and the typical student's grade point average has gone up. The conclusion; working with the strengths of others strengthens each individual who decides to make the effort. Students learn to work as part of a group during school and carry this skill to the workplace. Their expectation entering the workplace is that teamwork is the way work is done. Why? Because they have experienced how well it works.

Baseball legend Babe Ruth once said, "The way a team plays as a whole determines its success. You may have the greatest bunch of individual stars in the world, but if they don't play together, the club won't be worth a dime." Teamwork is the ability to work together toward a common vision and the ability to direct individual accomplishments toward organizational objectives. It is the fuel that allows uncommon results for both the organization and the individual.

Truth: Teams are "I"ndividuals focused on a common goal.

Simply put, when we say, "there is no I in team", we discourage people from participating and providing their best effort. For teamwork to work we need competent people on the team and these people must give their best effort to achieving the team's objectives.

If the "I"ndividuals on the team are to give their best effort, there must be some reward to do so. That reward comes in two forms. First is the pride and sense of accomplishment that comes from succeeding at a difficult mission. Whether it be winning a Super Bowl or bringing a world-class product to market, winning is a real rush! Second is the ability to realize one's own goals in the process.

The essential point that should be made about the "I" in team is that there is a synergy between achieving team goals and achieving individual goals. The two go hand in hand. When teamwork recognizes and pursues that synergy, both the team and the individual are the better for it. When teamwork denies that synergy, the most competent team members opt out, leaving teamwork in the hands of those poor souls who neither desire nor aspire to achieve.

How to make it work.

One of the fundamental elements of teamwork is role clarity. Traditionally, role has been defined as the contribution the team member is expected to make to the team. In order to capitalize on the synergy between team accomplishment and individual achievement, we surface another dimension of each team member's role. In the course of achieving the team's mission, what personal goals do you want to achieve?

I say we surface another dimension rather than we add a new dimension because the individual goals have always been present. When we fail to bring out those objectives as part of a team member's role, they can come in conflict with achieving the team's mission. By surfacing individual goals, we make them honest and validate them; we reduce the likelihood of conflict and increase the likelihood of achieving both team and individual goals.

In the football analogy, a running back may have a personal goal of averaging 100 yards or more per game. As the team pursues its mission of winning a championship, there will be some games where the running game is shut down and the team will turn to the passing attack. In that game the running back may only get 50 yards. However, in the next game, as the defense focuses on stopping the passing game, that same running back will have the opportunity to run for 150 yards. Both the team and the running back achieve their goals.

In the business environment, a product development team may have the mission of capturing market share through new product introductions to the market. A contributor from a functional discipline (sales, marketing, engineering, manufacturing, etc.) may have a personal goal to advance their career by gaining exposure to other business disciplines or by leading the effort in their discipline to advance market share. Either way, the goals are synergistic.

A team does not have role clarity until every team member knows two things about every other team member:

1. The contribution the team member is expected to make to the team.

2. The personal goals the team member seeks to achieve.

Once both issues are clarified, each "I" on the team will be free to pursue the synergistic success of teamwork without hidden agendas.

Careful attention is also required to the formal reward system of the organization. Any time that the formal reward system (compensation, bonuses, perquisites, recognition, etc,) is in conflict with the team's mission or goals, the formal reward system will encourage behavior antithetical to the mission. This makes it virtually impossible to focus effort on common goals. Lets face it, if your mission is to maximize efficiency across the organization but your compensation is based on how many people report to you, you're going to maximize the number of people reporting to you regardless of the impact on efficiency.

"The credit belongs to the man who is actually in the arena, whose face is marred by dust
and sweat and blood; who strives valiantly;
who errs and comes short again and again,
who knows the great enthusiasms, the great
devotions, and spends himself in a worthy
cause; who at best, knows the triumph of high
achievement; and who, at the worst, if he fails,
at least fails while daring greatly, so that his
place shall never be with those cold and timid
souls who know neither victory nor defeat."

~ Theodore Roosevelt (1858 - 1919), "Citizen in a
Republic" April 23, 1910

"We should have teams only
use consensus to make
decisions."

"Oh no, that would grind
everything to a halt. Teams use
consensus techniques, the
process of exchanging points of
view and listening for
understanding, to make many
different types of decisions."

Chapter 7

Teams make consensus decisions

The most troublesome lie.

A Fairy Tale

As teamwork became the way of things in the world of work, it came to pass that teams made more decisions. Therefore, fewer decisions were brought to the powers that be for their council. This was threatening to those whose power came from decision authority. If the people of the kingdom did not have to come to them for decisions, soon they would not come to them at all!

"Isn't there something we can do to keep them from making decisions?" one petty sorcerer wondered aloud. "We could bog them down in the process," replied another. "Why, whatever do you mean?" queried the first.

By and by, they sought the advice of the team trainer. Edicts were issued requiring that consensus be taught as the only correct decision methodology. The team trainer then taught a decision process where team members argued their positions and pleaded their cases. Others parried and offered dissenting opinions. It was taught that consensus required all to agree with the decision and many refused to compromise. The most important group decision making skill, listening, was neither taught nor encouraged. Few listened and the process slowly ground to a halt.

The Real World

One thing you can be sure will always be included in a team training session is a consensus decision-making exercise. The basic drill is always the same. The team is required to gain consensus on a list of items. It may be a survival scenario, a project management exercise, or even the order in which jurors vote not guilty in the classic film *Twelve Angry Men*. Regardless, there are always those stupid items the team must prioritize. The exercise usually is scheduled to take from two to four hours and participants are told they are not permitted to vote. No one ever seems to realize that, were the survival scenarios real, by the time the decision is made everyone would already be dead.

Participants are instructed to keep at it until they achieve consensus – a state of mutual agreement addressing all legitimate concerns of group members that permits all to support the decision. Then, in virtually all exercises, the individual and team answers are scored against an expert's opinion.

You've got it; we use a single expert opinion as the benchmark to "prove" consensus is the best decision method.

The lie of consensus decision-making rests on the direction not to vote and on the implication that this is the process by which teams make decisions. First, even if no formal vote is taken, team members cast a vote in many ways. They will choose to give in just to get the exercise over with, thereby voting for a position they do not actually support. They will agree to support another person's position in one instance if the other person will support theirs in another instance. This is a form of the you-scratch-my-back-and-I'll-scratch-yours behavior fundamental to getting things done in most organizations. Second, you will never see a consensus of all of the people impacted by a decision. In organizations of 10 to 300,000+ associates, any associate left out of the decision process will not have been part of the consensus. Even in a group of eight people, it is virtually impossible to achieve true consensus. Rather, what you will achieve is an informed vote that all will support. Informed because all had an opportunity to present their point of view before the vote was cast and supported for the same reason.

Tom Ross, a friend of mine who is an IBEW journeyman electrician, was recently required to participate in a series of team training sessions conducted by a local college professor. After attending a couple of sessions, he said to me, "You're a management consultant aren't you? I sure hope you aren't peddling the same crap this guy is!" When I asked for more information, Tom told me the trainer had spent six hours on consensus decision-making. "This fool expects me to sit with my two apprentices and agree to the best way to do a conduit run! Hell, if I didn't know the best way to do a conduit run I wouldn't be a journeyman. This idiot couldn't even carry my tool box!"

When Peter Drucker wrote, "Most of what we call management consists of making it difficult for people to get their work done." He must have had folks like Tom Ross in mind! Tom's reaction is a classic example of the basic problem. Anytime you use training as a vehicle for organization change, the behaviors and skills advanced in the training session must be encouraged and reinforced in the workplace. If they are not, participants will perceive the training activity as one more instance of lip service and as a giant lie.

The reason we consider the consensus decision making lie to be the most troublesome is it is the one that is most obviously false. If one is told that consensus is a cornerstone of teamwork, and then doesn't know when to apply it, never sees it practiced, and also experiences decisions that clearly were made without use of consensus, then that person believes they were lied to. If consensus is a lie, then by association, everything else the company is saying about teamwork must also be a lie! Or, as Tom Ross put it, "I sure hope you aren't peddling the same crap this guy is!"

We live in an age where speed is a competitive weapon. Speed to market, speed of delivery, speed of response, speed, speed, speed. We also live in an age where quality is a competitive weapon. Customers want it fast, and they want it good. In this environment, teamwork must produce quality results with speed. That isn't done by consensus. IT

TAKES TOO LONG! Rather, effective team based organizations recognize and advocate the truth about team decision making.

Truth: Teams use consensus techniques to make four types of decisions.

Consensus techniques, the process of exchanging points of view and listening for understanding to each point of view, are used to achieve four types of decisions:

DECISION TYPES

- **Type I:** the leader makes a nonnegotiable decision without team input.

- **Type II:** the leader gathers team input and then makes an informed decision.

- **Type III**: the team makes the decision with the leader participating as an equal member.

- **Type IV**: the team makes the decision and takes action without involving the leader.

Every president and CEO I have interviewed characterized type II as his/her dominant decision type. For example, when Bob Eaton was running Chrysler Corporation, an article was published in the employee newsletter explaining that his primary decision approach was to solicit input from others and then make a decision on his own. Bruce Carbonari of Fortune Brands takes a slightly different approach. He makes a type I decision on some of the criteria the decision must meet, and then has his staff make a decision that will achieve the criteria. When Gene Winfeld ran the Kirby Company, he used his senior managers as a sounding board but held on to the authority to make the final decision. Eric Koik, of Komet of America often pursued a type III decision but reserved the final say for himself (type II). In fact, in every case, if the staff team can't or won't make a decision, the president/ CEO will. As the leader, that is their job.

It only stands to reason that an organization of several hundred or several thousand people will not poll everyone before making every decision. Consequently it is important that everyone in a team based organization understand that the vast majority of decisions in the organization will be made without their input. If people don't understand how decision making works, they will perceive type I to be the dominant decision type. Why? Because no matter how a decision is made, if you did not participate in it, it comes to you as a made decision. A nonnegotiable decision made without your input, no mater how it was made, looks an awful lot like a type I.

What makes a decision effective is a function of accuracy and implementation. Accuracy asks, "Was it the correct decision?" Implementation asks, "Did the people support it well enough to implement it?" Effective team organizations work to consciously involve and solicit input from a wide range of people. They also become very efficient at exchanging informed points of view. This increases accuracy by adding to the information base from which the decision is made. It improves the implementation by permitting those involved in implementing decisions to have input to the process. However, the goal is effectiveness, not consensus.

Attempting to achieve consensus usually accomplishes nothing other than grinding the wheels of progress to a halt.

How to make it work.

To clarify how teams and team based organizations make decisions, three components should be in place:

1. An easy method for establishing decision expectations.

2. Common decision logic.

3. Effective communication skills.

An easy method for establishing decision expectations.

In my client companies, we make type I, type II, type III, and type IV part of the jargon of the organization. This facilitates communication and understanding about what style of decision is being made. When a manager convenes a meeting, s/he will often begin by telling the group, "This is going to be a type III meeting." Everyone in the room then knows they are going to arrive at joint decisions where everyone has an equal vote, including the manager. When a team is having difficulty coming to closure on a course of action, the team leader will announce, "Ok, I'm going to type II this." The team knows the leader has heard the input and will make the decision. As you can see, creating common understanding around the "jargon" of decision types creates a vehicle for establishing expectations on how a decision will be made.

Common decision logic.

We then go to work on decision efficiency with training and reinforcement systems for a common decision logic process and robust communication skills. The basic logic flow is:

DECISION LOGIC

1. What decision is being made?

2. What criteria must the decision meet?

3. What other criteria are desirable to meet?

4. What alternatives can be identified?

5. How well does each alternative meet the established criteria?

6. What are the risks?

7. How do we manage the risks?

By applying a common logic, everyone in the organization understands the process and can participate more effectively. Team members receive training in decision making that focuses on applying the process to various decisions commonly encountered in the business and in their personal lives.

Effective communication skills.

The crowning piece of the puzzle is communication. The more effective team members are at understanding one another and explaining their point of view, the more efficient team decision making becomes. Therefore, we focus on skills to improve communication effectiveness. These are the same skills needed to form consensus. However, we are seeking communication effectiveness applied around decision logic. We are not seeking consensus. The fundamental communication skills are:

- Listen for understanding

- Exchange points of view

- Question for clarity

- Clarify understanding

- Establish closure

By providing teams a legitimate range of decision types, common decision logic, and efficient communication skills you make available an efficient, effective, and documented approach to team decision making. You also develop a strong base of people who are skilled decision makers and communicators.

"Indecision is like a stepchild: if he does not wash his hands, he is called dirty, if he does, he is wasting water."

~ African proverb

"Teamwork is about relationships."

"Teamwork is about results. Good relationship help achieve results but the focus must always be on results!"

Chapter 8

Teamwork is about relationships

The trainer's lie.

A Fairy Tale

Reward and punishment were hallmarks of the Kingdom of Work. Positive results were oftimes rewarded by the rulers of the kingdom. On the other hand, negative results were frowned upon, and a royal frown was never a good thing. The wondrous wizard formed teams around the issues and opportunities confronting the kingdom. They were focused on resolving these issues and capitalizing on the opportunities. As a result, they generated positive results and royal smiles. This was a good thing.

"Perhaps," one petty sorcerer mused, "we need a bit of misdirection. If teams continue to create positive results, they will win royal blessing and receive the rewards of the king-dom."

"What form of misdirection did you have in mind?" queried his partner.

"I was thinking of the Abilene Paradox."

"The Abilene Paradox?"

"Yes, it comes from an old movie about a group of folks so engaged in not offending one another that they won't speak up. There-fore they do the wrong things and generate atrocious results."

"Surely you jest. In my experience, it is easier to get things done if one gets along well with one's co-workers."

True, but not if the focus is getting along at the expense of getting results."

"You mean if we get teams to focus on getting along they will stop focusing on achieving positive results?"

"That's exactly what I mean!"

The Real World

Though it may be developed with the best of intentions, most of what passes for "team building" stresses good relationships so heavily that partici-pants in the team building activity leave with the perception that teamwork is about relationships. It is true that people who have good interpersonal relations are more facile at gaining results than those who do not. However, the secret to good relationships in a team environment is open and honest communication. When "getting along" becomes the hallmark of teamwork, teams go into "play nicely in the sandbox" mode. In this mode, fear of offending someone causes open and honest communications to stop. Without open and honest communication, teamwork fails to produce results.

A recent incident at a major package delivery company illustrates the point. A brand new sales representative succeeded in getting a $500,000 piece of business that would normally have gone to another package delivery company. To insure timely delivery and first class service, the customer was paying the company's highest shipping rate. So the shipment was at the company's highest margin. Better yet, this was the first of what would be many shipments if the "trial order" went well.

As soon as she knew the order was coming, the sales representative gave her manager advanced warning of the shipment. To be sure the order was handled well, the sales manager sent email messages and made several telephone calls to the people who would have to process the shipment. This was done in an effort to give the operations side of the business ample notice of the size and importance of the consignment. Further, the shipping labels to be used were tested in advance to insure they were machine readable. This would facilitate handling the order once it arrived at the distribution center.

The shipment entered the package delivery company's system on Friday and should have gone out the same day. Four days later, on Tuesday, the new sales representative had the opportunity to tour the distribution center. While on the tour, she discovered almost two dozen pallets of her $500,000 pilot order sitting in a corner of the center not being processed. She asked a supervisor why the shipment was still there when it should have been gone three days ago. The supervisor answered, "Don't worry, it's not dated so it shouldn't really matter." The rep then called her sales manager for help.

When the sales manager called the distribution center manager he was told there had been a problem reading the shipping labels by machine. (Remember that the labels had been tested for machine readability.) Further, there had been a security problem the day before and the entire distribution center staff was exhausted from dealing with it. The attitude was, "What's the big deal, the material wasn't dated so we'll get around to it." At this point, the sales manager went over the distribution manager's head to garner the executive clout needed to get the shipment moving.

The following day the distribution center manager sent an email to the sales manager saying,

> "It's real nice to know we are a team here. Your actions are disheartening and divisive and not at all in keeping with our team spirit. Please don't ever talk to me about teamwork again if you are going to act the way you did."

The distribution manager is guilty of many things, the least of which is hiding behind the "teamwork is about relationships" lie. He wants the understanding of teamwork to be limited to believing that it requires being nice to each other even if the job is not getting done. Unfortunately, this is not an isolated incident. In the course of the research for this book, I heard this same story over and over again. The cast of players changed. The company changed. The exact situation changed.

However, the message was always the same, "Teamwork means we have to like each other and play nicely together. Results aren't important."

The reality is that there is no reason to have teamwork other than to accomplish results. If teamwork is to succeed, everyone involved needs to understand the truth about teamwork.

Truth: Teamwork is about results.

The primary focus of teamwork must be on accomplishing results – the team's mission and goals. Think about your own experience, and you will realize that relationships alone will not sustain any team. I've asked hundreds of people to give me an example of any teamwork activity they are involved in. The answers encompass work, social, and community activities and all have one thing in common, goals to be achieved!

You're in a bowling league. What keeps the bowling team together, the relationships or the bowling? You're heavily involved in politics. What keeps the team together, the relationships or the political campaigns? You're an elder/vestry member at your church, mosque, or synagogue. What keeps the team together, the relationships or the religious center? If you think it's the relationships, try taking away the bowling, politics, religious center and see what happens. The team will disband.

The only reason for using teamwork is to achieve results. Effective teams focus on achieving results and work toward relationships that support that accomplishment. The fact is that the only reason for teams to work on relationships is that groups working in harmony tend to achieve the best results.

I have a friend and associate who is an information technology consultant. Much of his work is done as a subcontractor to one of three larger consulting firms. As you might expect, these three firms typically compete against each other for the same contracts and their relationships are, at best, cordial. They usually perceive one another as the enemy.

All three consulting firms recently contacted my friend to inquire about his availability to participate in a telecommunications project. As it turns out, all three firms were pursuing the same project and not one of them had the full scope of resources needed to satisfy the project requirements. My friend recognized that, by working together, the three firms could satisfy all of the project's requirements. He orchestrated a meeting of principles from the three consultancies.

The meeting was polite but tense. None of the participants had reason to trust the others. In fact, even the location of the meeting had been a major bone of contention. My associate facilitated the discussion and laid out the requirements of the prospective telecommunications consulting assignment. Gradually, the three principles came to realize that their best chance at getting the assignment was to work together as a team, a group of people giving their best efforts to a common goal.

The three firms presented a joint proposal to conduct the consulting assignment. They still compete on other assignment and projects. They still have relationships that are cordial at best. However, they are achieving results together that no one of them could have achieved alone. I call that teamwork. It's about results, not relationships!

How to make it work.

The key to focusing on results is to put results first by defining everything in terms of the mission. The formula for team development has traditionally been mission, goals, roles, work process, and relationships. However, when teams have clarity of mission, common goals, and defined roles, the relationships tend to take care of themselves. Therefore, team development sessions need to emphasize mission, goals, and roles - not relationships. Team members do need to maintain open and honest communication about what each expects of the others, even if this communication creates conflict or is not perceived to be "nice." As such we modify the traditional approach to replace relationships with expectations. Further, all subordinate elements are defined in terms of the mission:

- **Mission**: a succinct statement of the overall result expected of the team.

- **Goals**: milestones leading to the accomplishment of the team's mission.

- **Roles**: the contribution each team member is expected to make to the mission and the personal goals the team member seeks to achieve.

- **Work processes**: common approaches to achieving the goals and mission.

- **Expectations**: ongoing, open, and honest communication among team members on what they expect of one another relative to achieving the mission.

Mission must be paramount.

When an organization places mission focus in the forefront people know exactly what they are supposed to be working on.

In the package delivery example above, either the organization had no meaningful mission or the distribution center manager had no concept of the organization's mission. Neither he nor his people were focused on package delivery. He was focused on keeping people happy and, in the absence of leadership, who knows what his people were focused on.

The irony is that by sacrificing achievement for happiness he lost both achievement and happiness. The only people less happy than those who fail to perform are those who fail to perform and get caught at it! By making the mission paramount the manager could have given his staff a sense of pride in accomplishment and built that pride across the organization. By focusing on relationships, he built neither pride nor relationships.

An interesting side note, the brand new sales person who brought in the $500,000 order was the top salesperson in her region for the quarter. She and the sales team accomplished significant goals in support of the company mission. They were ecstatic. Would you like to venture a guess as to how their relationships are?

Also, in the information technology telecommunications consulting example, the people involved are seeing their relationships build and improve as they work together in an effort to achieve common goals.

When teamwork is about results, when the mission and goals are clear, when everyone understands their role, relationships take care of themselves.

"Four vital signs give us a working definition of culture and tell us most of what we need to know about the operating state of any company.

1. Power: Do employees believe they can affect organizational performance? Do they believe they have the power to make things happen?

2. Identity: Do individuals identify rather narrowly with their professions, working teams, or functional units, or do they identify with the organization as a whole?

3. Conflict: How do members of the organization handle conflict? Do they smooth problems over, or do they confront and resolve them?

4. Learning: How does the organization learn? How does it deal with new ideas?"

~Richard Pascale, Mark Millemann, and Linda Gioja in "Changing the Way We Change"

"One thing is for sure. Teams will tie people up in more meetings."

"Actually, teamwork makes meetings more effective. As a result, there are usually fewer meetings."

Chapter 9

Teamwork requires more meetings

The great excuse not to begin.

A Fairy Tale

Rumor had it that a great meeting hall would be built in the Kingdom of Work. Surrounding the great meeting hall would be many major meeting halls and surrounding the major meeting halls would be minor meeting halls. Stories spread rapidly through the kingdom that teams would fill the many halls and all the people of the kingdom would be consumed doing the work of teamwork. This activity would devour the time of all the people, leaving not an instant to do 'real' work.

"But we already consume most of the people's time in meetings" said one petty sorcerer. "If we held no meetings, people would expect us to actually do something.

Meetings give us activity that keeps us busy without really accomplishing anything" "Yes, but now we can blame meetings on teamwork", replied another.

The Real World

The most common complaint heard in most organizations is that too much time is consumed by meaningless meetings. If you are like many professional/managerial employees, you spend approximately 40% of your time in some type of meeting. There is the weekly staff meeting, the budget review meeting, the meeting to plan the company outing, meetings to recognize things, to update people, to get your input on something, to investigate something else, to respond to another thing. The one thing most of these meetings have in common is that they accomplish little or nothing. As a result, additional meetings are held on the same issue or topic.

Ask yourself three questions:
1. In a typical work week, how much of your time is spent in meetings?

2. How many of the meetings simply rehashed what had been discussed in a previous meeting on the same topic?

3. How often was anything actually accomplished by or in the meeting?

For most of us the answers are: 1) too much, 2) most of them, and 3) not very often.

As I began writing this chapter, I spoke on the phone with a prospective client who spent the entire previous week in a senior management meeting. I asked what they accomplished, and she gave me a laundry list of the presentations given at the meeting. My response was "Yes, but what was accomplished?" After some reflection, the prospective client said, "Can I count a sore bottom as an accomplishment?"

This company had tied up their entire management staff for five full days and the net result of the five day meeting was a lot of sore backsides and bored people. Just to check the validity of this assumption I asked a couple of other questions:

Q: Did you learn anything you didn't already know?
A: No.

Q: Were any decisions made?
A: No

Q: Did you resolve any unresolved issues?
A: No, but we reviewed and discussed several.

Q: Had these issues been reviewed and discussed before?
A: Yes.

Q: Was anyone recognized or rewarded during the meetings?
A: No, but each operating unit gave an update of their progress toward goals.

Q: Was this new information to anyone?
A: No.

Regrettably, this conversation can be held following most corporate meetings. As a result, most people have no desire to attend additional meetings, and one of the frequent objections to teamwork is that it will require more meetings. Why this objection? Because the typical business meeting is a waste of time for most meeting participants.

In a conventional scenario, people from various parts of the organization attend a meeting. These participants may have a legitimate interest in the topic or purpose of the meeting but also have plenty to do on their everyday jobs. The added burden of whatever the meeting is about, is simply one more distraction. As a result, the commitment to the objectives of the meeting is, at best, limited. During the meeting, participants are reluctant to add to their personal work load by stepping up to the issues of the meeting.

In reality, teams do have meetings. However, because teams have clear missions to pursue and goals to achieve, team meetings tend to produce results. Further, because they produce results, a team may meet once or twice to resolve an issue that the organization has been holding meetings on for years!

General Signal's Near Manufacturing unit in Ohio provides a good example. The business grew up as an independently owned company run by the founder's son-in-law. When General Signal acquired the business it was evident that there was significant opportunity for improving the material flow in the manufacturing process. General Signal hired a consulting firm to examine the issue. In the course of their examination, the consulting firm held many employee meetings and those meetings surfaced hundreds of improvement opportunities beyond material flow changes. Faced with this myriad of opportunities, the consulting study dragged on and on with meeting after meeting and no results. Opportunities were discussed but no action was taken.

Challenged as to the lack of results, the consultants said they didn't want to disrupt the process with "piecemeal" improvements. Rather, they wanted to define a holistic solution that harvested the lions share of the available opportunities to improve. Unfortunately for the consulting firm, teamwork happened!

A group of employees, frustrated by the never ending material flow issues, took it on themselves to do something. In a "gripe" session with their supervisor they said they could have addressed the material flow problem in a one hour meeting and implement the solution in two shifts. The supervisor took them up on the comment. The team met that evening and developed a new shop floor layout. They divided the implementation into three parts, 1) do ourselves by rearranging, 2) do ourselves with capital investment, and 3) requires an outside contractor.

The following day they presented their proposal to management and received approval to proceed with everything they could do themselves. In one meeting, a team of employees had accomplished what months of meetings had failed to achieve!

Truth: Teamwork makes meetings more effective.

In a team environment, meetings become more effective for two primary reasons:

1. The participants in the meeting have a shared interest and commitment to the outcomes of the meeting.

2. The same core elements that make teamwork effective make meetings effective.

The participants in the meeting have a shared interest and commitment to the outcomes of the meeting.

Members of teams share common missions and common goals. Team meetings focus on issues relevant to the shared mission and shared goals. As a result, participant commitment to achieving the purpose and desired outcomes of the meeting is significantly increased.

The Near Manufacturing team mentioned above had a high level of commitment to improving material flow in the plant. These employees took great pride in their work and were extremely frustrated with the situation that existed. The issue directly effected their jobs everyday. As a result, they were motivated and focused on a common mission. The earlier meetings had lost focus, and the ever expanding scope dragged the project out.

For many years design engineers at Moen Incorporated reinvented various elements of the faucet with each new design. The company wanted to achieve some commonality of components to improve manufacturing efficiency and reduce cost. Over more than three years, meetings were held on the topic of "design modularity". Over and over the question was asked "How can we use modular components across the product line to standardize manufacturing and reduce cost?" Many meetings were held but few built on the last and most revisited the issue without making progress. Frustrated with the lack of movement, the Vice President Marketing formed a team of design engineers and sales people to address the issue. In a single year the team developed a modular platform. The concept permitted the same components to be used in all non-visible areas of the faucet and the visible portion to be changed to suit the taste and design preference of the consumer. Yes, the team held meetings. However, rather than meeting for the sake of meeting, each meeting took the team a step closer to the goal.

The same core elements that make teamwork effective make meetings effective.

In earlier chapters I mentioned the five elements of effective teamwork: mission, goals, roles, work processes, expectations. There are also five elements of effective meetings and, while meeting managers use different terminology, the elements are the same. A good meeting has: a clear purpose, expected outcomes, participant selection and preparation, an agenda, and ground rules. Lets examine these compared to team elements:

MEETING	TEAM
Purpose	The mission of the meeting.
Outcomes	The goals the meeting will achieve.
Participant selection and preparation	The role of each participant.
Agenda	The work process for the meeting.
Ground Rules	Expectations for the meeting.

As you can see, the elements of a good meeting are the same elements that form good teams. Not only is every meeting an opportunity to effect teamwork, but organizations founded in the principles of teamwork effect good meetings.

How to make it work.

The primary point of this chapter is that, with or without teamwork, meetings happen. With teamwork meeting are more likely to achieve results because of focus, process, and follow-through.

Focus comes from the teams legitimate commitment to accomplishing the purpose and outcomes established for the meeting. Process is the five elements of effective teamwork practiced in each meeting. Follow-through comes from clearly defined roles and accountabilities. Even in environments that are not team based, meetings can be made more effective by practicing the five elements of effective teamwork in each and every meeting. That is:

1. **Mission**: no meeting should ever be held unless it has a clearly defined purpose. Purpose tells us why the meeting is being held and gives a prime focus for action.

2. **Goals**: before any meeting begins the expected outcome of the meeting should be defined in terms that clearly establish what is expected to be accomplished by the end of the meeting.

3. **Roles**: each meeting participant needs to know why they are attending and what they are expected to contribute to the meeting.

4. **Process**: given a clear purpose, defined outcomes, and participant roles, you now need to develop an agenda that will accomplish the outcomes in the time allotted.

Under no circumstances should an agenda ever be developed without first defining the purpose and outcomes of the meeting.

5. **Expectations**: every meeting needs ground rules that establish the expectations on how the meeting will be conducted and what is/is not expected of all participants.

Applying this approach to meetings will make the meetings effective and model the fundamentals of teamwork at the same time.

We also recommend a straight forward format for meeting minutes that incorporates the team approach and helps the meeting focus on three elements:

1. Purpose and desired outcome.

2. Decisions made.

3. Action items and accountability.

The following page shows this format for meeting minutes.

Three keys create meeting results, and thereby reduce the total number of meetings. These are focus, process, and follow-through. The teamwork elements of mission, goals, roles, process, and expectations provide the focus needed. Meeting agendas designed to accomplish the stated purpose and outcomes provide process. Meeting minutes compliment process. The last items on the minutes format are a review of accomplishments and planned next accomplishments. If you review accomplishments at the end of a meeting and you don't have any, you just ran a worthless meeting! STOP and honestly question what caused the failure.

MEETING MINUTES

Meeting Location: Date/Time:

Meeting Purpose:

Planned Outcomes:

Participants:

Decisions Made:

1.

2.

3.

4.

5.

Action Items:

Action	Person Accountable	Due Date

Accomplished this meeting:

Next planned accomplishments:

Next Meeting:

Meeting minutes not only compliment process but also support the last key, follow-through. Nothing happens unless the individuals responsible for action items fulfill the assignments. Once again, we come back to the fundamental truth that teams are groups of individuals focused on a common goal. As we'll see in the next chapter, for teamwork to work, each individual must do the work he or she is assigned. We track action items so that the team can follow-up on individual accountabilities.

"Meetings are a great trap. Soon you find yourself trying to get agreement and then the people who disagree come to think they have a right to be persuaded.... However, they are indispensable when you don't want to do anything."

~ John Kenneth Galbraith (b. 1908), U.S. economist. Ambassador's Journal, ch. 5, entry for April 22, 1969.

"At least we should agree that teams do work."

"In truth, for work to get done individual team members must do it. Teams think, team members do work."

Chapter 10

Teams do work

The slacker's lie.

A Fairy Tale

There is much work to be done in the Kingdom of Work, hence the name. Oh, there is time for politics and time to play but there is much work to be done. Yes, yes much work to be done. By now, you know that getting results is the reason the wondrous wizard brought teamwork to the kingdom. It is really about getting work done. Work, work, work. Yes that is what it is all about! Why, if it were not for work, there would be no reason for the kingdom to exist.

"That is what the petty sorcerers would have you believe," advised the wondrous wizard. "See how easily they shift from results to work. All that was needed was to make the connection. Now you can get lost in the activity (work) and lose track of the purpose of the activity (results)."

And the petty sorcerers cheered, "Ah, the power of the misdirection spell. Get them focused on the wrong thing. That's the ticket!"

The Real World

The thought that teams do work provides an interesting diversion from the purpose of teamwork. Obviously, there is a connection between accomplishing results and doing the work necessary to produce the desired outcomes. For anything to happen, team members must do work. However, the power of teamwork rests in the ability to coordinate work toward a common goal, thereby producing results. Although there is a cause and effect relationship, work and accomplishment are not the same.

I live on the shores of Lake Erie, a lake notorious for erosion along its southern shore. We recently installed a sea wall to protect our property from this erosion. We selected a sea wall over other means of erosion protection because we also wanted to install a davit capable of lifting a small boat out of the water and to provide a deck on which to store the boat. Think of all the work involved in this project. You have to prepare the foundation, build forms, mix concrete, set blocks, and many other chores. More importantly, all of this must be done in the correct sequence and several tasks have to come together at the right time.

The team of workers who built the wall did a very good job with one small hitch. As the crew poured concrete into the forms for the davit mount, the bolts that had to be embedded in the concrete were nowhere to be found. Someone had to make a mad dash to the hardware store to get the bolts before the concrete set. Fortunately the hardware store was close by, and they had the bolts in stock.

What happened? The team had, for the most part, performed flawlessly. The tasks were planned well. The forms were built at the right time and in the right place. The concrete was correctly mixed and there when it was needed. The seawall blocks had been laid for the foundation and the concrete cap had been poured. However, no one on the team had brought the davit mounting bolts, a simple bit of work that was necessary to accomplish the desired results. As it turns out, the team had done its job. They had analyzed the situation and selected an appropriate solution. They had planned the implementation thoroughly, coordinated their activities, and made decisions to facilitate the construction of the seawall and davit mount. There was significant information exchange as the project proceeded. The materials list included the davit bolts. In fact, the contractor himself had accepted the assignment of procuring the bolts. However, one person had failed to follow-through on an assigned task. The contractor had not procured the bolts. Even so, the team was able to exercise the communication, decision making, and flexibility to achieve the desired results.

My point is that, by focusing on the desired outcomes, the team had laid out a plan to achieve those results. However, for any work to get done, some individual has to do it! When a team member neglected to do a bit of assigned work needed to accomplish the desired result, the team arrived at a solution to the problem and implemented it. The implementation (keep the concrete from setting while someone gets the bolts) required individual team members to do coordinated work. The team develops plans and solutions, but the work to implement plans and solutions is done by individual team members, not the team.

The same is true in the omnipresent sports analogies surrounding teamwork. The work is coordinated and team members work together to achieve desired results. However, each team member must do the work assigned to them. The center has to snap the football to the quarterback who has to fake a handoff to the running back, who has to feign an off tackle run, while the quarterback passes the ball to a receiver who must catch the pass.

Truth: Teams think, team members do work.

The truth is that team members actually do all the work! It requires the effort of some individual (there's that darn "I" in team again) to actually make anything happen. If we allow the organization to believe that teams actually do work, we create an environment where individuals can shirk responsibility and accountability by hiding behind the team. "It wasn't my job, the team was supposed to do it!" We also lose the great power of teamwork ... the ability to focus collective mental power on solving a problem.

We have seen geometric increases in productivity in the past few years due to better thinking, not more work. In fact, increases in productivity are the only thing that gives true improvement in our standard of living. And, an increase in productivity by definition is accomplishing results with **less** work! What teams do is increase productivity. Work must be done but it is work with a purpose that is done by individual team members. The petty sorcerers of the world would have you believe that work is an end in itself. In reality, it is only the results that count. Who really cares if you work harder and accomplish nothing? Teamwork permits people to work smarter and accomplish more, often with less effort.

One of my favorite examples is the United States Postal Service (USPS). USPS offers Express Mail service that guarantees two-day delivery by 6:00 p.m. They have a customer in Ohio who has figured out that the USPS system can't make good on that promise for shipments to Hawaii. Once a week this customer ships a parcel to his son in Hawaii via express mail. He pays the postage of about $30.00 and the package takes more than two days to arrive. The next week he walks into the post office to get his refund and ship the next package. Free delivery to Hawaii from Ohio, not bad!

The most effective use of teams is to analyze situations, problem solve, plan, brain storm, coordinate, make decisions, exchange information, and follow-up/review progress. This two-day delivery issue is a classic opportunity to use teamwork effectively, and the effective teamwork response to this issue is to focus a team of folks on determining how to meet the two-day delivery guarantee. All three of USPS' major competitors are able to meet the two-day standard. Therefore, if USPS is to compete effectively (and stop shipping to Hawaii for free), they need to identify and put in place a process that supports the delivery guarantee. Unfortunately, USPS believes that teamwork is about doing work, so they tried working harder. However, no matter how hard the postal employees in Ohio worked, their effort still did not get the mail to Hawaii in two days.

Rather than recognize the power of teams to solve problems and deliver results, USPS believes teamwork is about teams doing work and playing nicely in the sandbox, that it is not ok to point out our shortcomings. As a result, one manager's proposed solution to this problem was to eliminate Hawaii from the two-day delivery guarantee. Recognizing this would put them at a competitive disadvantage, they chose to simply not include these zip codes in management performance measures. Heaven forbid they should hold themselves accountable to a performance standard that all of their major competitors can meet. In the end, USPS chose to ignore the problem and eliminate the Hawaii zipcode from their management performance measures.

Midas Incorporated provides a positive example. Midas established its reputation by offering a lifetime guarantee on replacement automobile mufflers. They were able to do this by building their mufflers with rust resistant stainless steel. As automobile manufacturers came under increasing pressure to improve quality, they began using stainless steel mufflers as original equipment. This virtually eliminated the aftermarket replacement business, which obviously had a severe impact on Midas' core business.

Midas management responded to this challenge by expanding the product offering to include brakes, steering, and suspension repair/replacement. The idea was to become the one-stop-shop for anything under the car. Then Midas began to exercise teamwork. They approached the problem by assembling a team of management members and franchisees. The team addressed the issue through a reinvention the business. They proposed refocusing it from "under the car" to "the auto service experts." The team envisioned a "New Midas", designed to make visiting Midas more enjoyable for customers. They wanted a new, brighter, contemporary look in refurbished shops. No longer just brakes and mufflers, Midas was to become a full service operation. All Midas shops would offer traditional Midas core services for exhaust, brakes, steering, and suspension. They would also offer new categories of drive train, starting and charging, batteries, climate control and maintenance services, such as oil changes, filters, belts, wiper blades and radiator flush and fill. In addition, the "New Midas" program would include standards for employee technical certification and appearance, and expanded hours of operation.

The team envisioned the reinvention. However, it would take a lot of work to accomplish it, and the work would have to be done by individual franchisees. Each franchisee, an independent business owner, would need to make substantial investment in his or her business to change the face of Midas. The team could and did sell the concept. The team could and did orchestrate the process of implementation. The team could and did define the new business paradigm. The team could not and did not do all the work needed to accomplish the transformation. Individual team members did this. Two thousand seven hundred independent franchisees and their employees did it all, working on a common vision to reinvent the business.

How to make it work.

The "teams do work" lie is a bit more subtle than the other seven lies. Work must be done to accomplish anything. However, when teams view work as the end result, they lose sight of the goal and nothing gets accomplished. The key to managing this lie is to understand two things:

- Team focus must **always** be on accomplishing desired results.

- Accountable individuals do the actual work.

Team focus must always be on accomplishing desired results.

Never forget that the basic definition of a team is "a group of people **focused on a common goal**." Any time the focus of the team is distracted from the common goal the team becomes less effective. Even if the distraction is to focus on work. When focused on work the team loses sight of the forest for the trees.

To maintain focus on the goal, team energy is invested in defining, planning, and organizing the work that needs to be done and in solving problems confronted along the way. If the team is involved in something other than analyzing situations, problem solving, planning, brainstorming, coordinating, making decisions, or exchange of information, it has probably lost focus on the end results!

Accountable individuals do actual work.

No work gets done if some individual does not do it. As such every action item the team establishes must include clearly identified accountability – who is going to actually make sure it gets done?

You'll recall we recommended a simple format for meeting minutes in the last chapter. The last portion of the meeting minutes format was action items with defined accountability and timelines. It looks like this:

Action	Person Accountable	Due Date
1. Get davit bolts	B. Vatruba	July 10
2. Schedule concrete	A. Rod	July 6

By maintaining an action item list (and following up on it), teams insure that the work that needs to get done gets done. In combination with the continuous role clarification mentioned earlier, this simple process helps team members know what is expected of them on an ongoing basis. It teaches team members that no work gets done unless someone accepts the accountability for doing it.

In order for the team to analyze information, some member must gather it. In order for the team to implement an action plan, individual members must do each task in the plan. In order for ...

"Nothing will work unless you do."

~ Maya Angelou, poet, educator, historian, author

Teamwork is the way we do business.

Management is shared - leadership is the responsibility of the executive team.

The executive sponsor has prime responsibility for team success.

Teams are "I"ndividuals focused on a common goal.

Teams use consensus techniques to make four types of decisions.

Teamwork is about results.

Teamwork makes meetings more effective.

Teams think, team members do work.

Chapter 11

The eight truths

A summary of the truths of teamwork.

A Fairy Tale

Amongst the petty sorcerers there was great concern, for theirs was the labor of those threatened with extinction. Should the wonderous wizard succeed and teamwork become the way of the world, where would they get their power? How could they maintain their fiefdoms? What reason would people have to show them deference? They had woven their web well. Deceit provided the warp and lies the woof of the tapestry they wove as a defense against teamwork. But, still they worried. They had brought all of their skills to bear on the powers of teamwork, but what if the truths became known?

The Real World

For each of the eight lies of teamwork, I have offered a corresponding truth and some guidance on how to make the truth flourish in your organization. Be warned, petty sorcerers do not give up easily. The price of effective teamwork, as with any freedom, is eternal vigilance. When vigilance fails, the organization regresses. This regression is fed not only by inattention but also by the continuous efforts of the petty sorcerers, those who seek power for its own sake and glory only in their own ego gratification. Let's review the truths.

Truth: Teamwork is the way we do business.

There is no good reason to use teamwork if it is not focused on accomplishing the needs of the organization. To accomplish the needs of the organization, teamwork cannot be outside the business, it must be the way we do business. I offer three steps to accomplish this.

1. Focus teamwork efforts on issues that are important to the business.

2. Establish executive sponsorship.

3. Empower teams to implement decisions within defined boundaries.

Petty sorcerers will seek to focus your teams in other arenas. They would have you set teams up for things less consequential as a "learning experience" and to "give them experience". They would have you believe that sponsorship is inappropriate use of executive time. And, they would have you believe implementation needs their enlightened oversight.

What better use is there of an executives time than insuring the organization is addressing the needs of the business? Sponsorship is a misallocation of executive effort only when petty sorcerers succeed in having teams focused away from the needs of the business. As to implementation oversight, it is usually nothing more than obstruction (the ability to stop progress toward defined goals) or management by passing notes (the ability to pass what is happening along to the next level of management).

Truth: Management is shared – leadership is the responsibility of the executive team.

Never confuse leadership with management or supervision. Leadership establishes the direction of the organization and the culture that permits the organization to excel. Self directed teams can take the organization in leadership's direction and implement the desired culture if three fundamentals are in place:

1. Teams are structured to accomplish the initiatives and goals established by the strategic plan.

2. Teamwork is viewed as a critical process in the organization, requiring continuous process improvement and process discipline.

3. The supervisor's role is reoriented to coaching, teaching, building teams, and creating a climate for performance.

By confusing management with leadership, petty sorcerers create a lack of focus and confuse the goals and direction of the organization. Teamwork is often threatening to managers and supervisors because self-directed teams can be self-managed and self-supervised. As a result, it is critical to understand the role of managers and supervisors in a team based organization.

Managers still oversee resource allocation, process improvement, process discipline, and goal setting within strategic initiatives. However they allocate resources across multiple teams, they process improve teamwork, and above all they exercise process discipline on teamwork.

Supervisors are the first line of process improvement for teamwork. They coach and teach the skills and knowledge needed to succeed in the organization. They build the teams used to accomplish goals. And they create a climate for performance by reinforcing the desired culture of the organization.

Truth: The executive sponsor has prime responsibility for team success.

The keys to the success of any organization design are accountability and empowerment. For any organizational unit to be effective it must be empowered to accomplish its purpose and goals. Teamwork is no different. A team must be empowered to accomplish its purpose (mission) and goals. Empowerment is the role of the executive sponsor and, regardless of the organization design, unless this role is fulfilled, the organization is destined to fail. I identified three basic elements for team sponsorship:

1. Assign a management/executive sponsor to every team.

2. Hold the sponsor accountable for the success of the team.

3. Hold team kick off and team progress sessions with the sponsor.

In truth, these elements apply to any organization structure. The petty sorcerer would have you believe they do not apply to teams. That way teamwork can be set up to fail. Executives must have ultimate accountability for the success or failure of the organization and accomplishment of the organization's goals. They enhance the potential for success by empowering the organization with enablement, definition, freedom to perform, and advocacy.

Truth: Teams are "I"ndividuals focused on a common goal.

I was reading the local paper the other day and saw a full page advertisement with a huge banner. You guessed it, the banner said "THERE IS NO I IN TEAM" I swear, if I hear this one more time I'll puke! The basic definition of a team is "a group of people (read individuals) focused on a common goal. If there is no "I" in team, there is no team.

The petty sorcerer would have you believe individual contributions do not count and individuals cannot achieve personal goals as members of teams. I suggest they look at the US Special Forces teams. They are made up of highly skilled individuals each achieving personal goals as a part of a crack team of experts. They model the role clarity I propose where every team member knows two things about every other team member:

1. The contribution the team member is expected to make to the team.

2. The personal goals the team member seeks to achieve.

Truth: Teams use consensus techniques to make four types of decisions.

The process of consensus decision making is taught in team training sessions because it encompasses several basic skills designed to make teams more effective. These are: listen for understanding, exchange points of view, question for clarity, clarify understanding, and establish closure. Unfortunately, teams and team based organizations never actually use consensus, it takes too long. To have team members believe otherwise is a lie.

The petty sorcerer would grind action to a halt by insisting on complete consensus. The use of consensus skills (listen, exchange points of view, question, clarify, close) to achieve a majority or minority decision is more efficient and effective. I have provided three components to clarify how teams and team based organizations make decisions:

1. An easy method for establishing decision expectations (type I, type II, type III, and type IV).

2. Common decision logic.

3. Effective communication skills.

Team training needs to teach the skills taught in consensus decision making while removing the expectation that consensus can or should be the norm.

Truth: Teamwork is about results.

When teamwork is about results, when the mission and goals are clear, when everyone understands their role, relationships take care of themselves. Therefore, we need to focus on mission goals, and roles.

The petty sorcerer loves relationships. They're warm and fuzzy. They make everyone feel good, They're fun! And, with a little subterfuge, they can distract the team from actually doing anything productive. However relationships only matter in the context of the mission and goals. If the team is not focused on the achievement of a common goal, it is, by definition, not a team!

Truth: Teamwork makes meetings more effective.

The rallying cry of the petty sorcerer is that teamwork will consume the organization in meetings. This lie is effective only because the organization is already consumed in meetings and members of the organization have no desire to participate in any meeting that wastes time.

With or without teamwork, meetings happen. For meetings to produce results, they require focus, process, and follow-through. Teams, bring these three element to bare in meetings. As a result, team meetings are more likely to achieve results, thereby eliminating the need for further meetings on the same topic.

Wonder of wonders, teamwork reduces the number of meetings! How, by actually accomplishing results.

I've provided an approach that improves your meetings by using the five elements of effective teams in every meeting. Note: A meeting is a group of people. A meeting with clear goals is a group of people with a common goal, a team. Therefore every meeting is an opportunity to practice teamwork. You do this by insuring the meeting has a clear purpose, clearly defined expected outcomes, participant selection and preparation, an agenda to achieve the desired outcomes, and ground rules to establish expectations.

Truth: Teams think, team members do work.

Last, but certainly not least, the thought that teams do work is too easily used to accomplish two subterfuges:

1. By making work the focus, work can be pursued as an end in itself rather than a means to an end.

2. By making the team responsible for work, incompetent or lazy individuals can hide their incompetence or laziness behind the team.

When teams view work as the end result, they lose sight of the mission and nothing gets accomplished. When individuals expect the team to do work, they don't do work themselves.

Teams must focus on results. They think through how to achieve results and individual team members do the work necessary. Petty sorcerers would rather you did not understand:

- Team focus must **always** be on accomplishing desired results.

- Accountable individuals do actual work.

"It is a pleasure to stand upon the shore, and to see ships tost upon the sea: a pleasure to stand in the window of a castle, and to see a battle and the adventures thereof below: but no pleasure is comparable to standing upon the vantage ground of truth... and to see the errors, and wanderings, and mists, and tempests, in the vale below."

~ Sir Francis Bacon (1561 - 1626) essayest and author

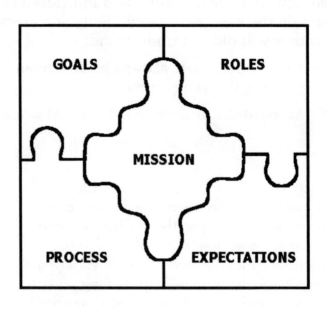

"There are five basic elements to the teamwork puzzle."

Chapter 12

Five elements of effective teams

Basic team formation.

A Fairy Tale

The wondrous wizard stood puzzling over the book of spells and incantations, "A touch of this, a twist of that, pieces from here and snatches from there" he declared. "The formula has become too complex!"

As teamwork grew in the kingdom, petty sorcerers had been about the business of adding layers of complexity to teamwork that need not exist. They reasoned that, as with all things, the more complex the matter became the less useful it would be. Besides, complexity gave them new avenues for empire. Someone had to be the keeper of complex things. What better role for a petty sorcerer than that?

A splendid white light surrounded the wizard as he raised his staff. Fire and lightning spewed forth from the staff unraveling all the complexities before it and leaving only five elements for effective teams: mission, goals, roles, process, and expectations.

The Real World

In previous chapters I have made reference to the five elements of effective teams: mission, goals, roles, process, and expectations. Having started on the path, teams and teamwork are built following the guidelines outlined in chapter 11 and focusing on the five elements of effective teams. Let us add definition to these elements and provide a few insights and approaches to help with each of them.

Mission provides the focus for all activity.

A team is a group of people focused on a common goal. The team's mission clearly defines the goal on which the team members are focused. There are several guidelines for an effective mission statement:

- Mission statements must be short. Preferably fewer than 15 words, never more than twenty words. This makes the mission something team members can remember and use for focus.

- Mission clearly states the team's reason for existing in specific terms.

- Mission is 100% what and 0% how. There is no reason to clutter the focus of a mission with how it will be accomplished. How is covered in goal statements and expectations.

- Team missions must be aligned with the mission and strategic initiatives of the organization.

- The mission should distinguish the team from other teams and inspire focused action.

Mission is absolutely critical to provide focus. Bob Nesbit, one of my associates, tells a story about working at Newport News Shipbuilding. Although I cannot vouch for its truth, it provides a wonderful example of the effectiveness of a good mission. The mission of the shipyard was:

> We build good ships. At a profit if we can, a loss if we must, but always good ships.

Bob was participating in a meeting at the facility and the discussion had gone off on a tangent unrelated to the meeting purpose. From the back of the room some one called out, "Is this about building good ships?" Answered by silence, the participant went on to say, "Then I suppose we ought to get back to building good ships." The meeting immediately came back on track. No one was offended because everyone in the room knew the mission and supported it.

Goals are the milestones en route to mission accomplishment.

Goals establish what must be achieved in order to accomplish the mission. Effective goals are:

- A road map to mission accomplishment.

- Written in clear and specific terms.

- Measurable or observable.

  - Measurable in terms of quality, cost, timeliness, or quantity.

  - Observable by touch, taste, smell, vision, hearing.

- Realistic: It can be done.

- Achievable: The team has access to the resources to do it.

- Dated for completion.

There is a flow to the development of a team sometimes called forming, storming, norming and performing. Teams begin with the question, "Why are we here? (forming)" They move on to, "Who has what authority? (storming)" Next teams question, "How do we get things done? (norming)". Once these questions are resolved the team can begin to perform (performing). The establishment of mission provides the team's primary reason for being. However, the "Why are we here?" question has not been answered until team members have established the team's goals. The initial team launch should be a working session where the team establishes its goals and defines roles. Role definition answers the question "Who has what authority?" This takes the team immediately to productive activity and moves it directly to the performing stage of development.

Roles establish expected individual contribution.

Roles define each individual team member's contribution to the team and the team's contribution to the individual. Clear roles:

- Define the contribution the team member is expected to make to mission accomplishment.

- Define the team member's personal goals.

- Establish what the team member needs from others in order to be successful.

- Defines the team member's power and authority.

- Include input from team members, sponsor, and stakeholders.

There is a classic story that goes around many organizations about a worker who had an idea on how to improve the process she was working on. The worker stopped her supervisor one day and said, "I've got an idea that might improve this operation." The supervisor stared at the employee in stunned silence for a moment before responding, "Forget that stuff, we didn't hire you to think." In a team-based environment, every team member has the responsibility to think and contribute his or her ideas. This is the true power of teamwork. It draws people from a broad spectrum of the organization and focuses their brainpower on change.

Process provides tools.

Having defined the team with mission, goals, and roles, process lets us know how the team accomplishes its tasks. Process provides the tools used by the team for:

- Planning
- Decision making
- Problem solving
- Ideation
- Meeting management
- Situation analysis, etc.

I have touched on meeting and decision making process in earlier chapters. While Entire books have been written on team processes, it is important to understand that process is both a blessing and a curse. It is a blessing because it provides common approaches and common language to allow the team to accomplish its mission and goals. If all team members use the same jargon and same approach for planning, planning goes more smoothly because everyone understands the process. If every team member uses the same jargon and same approach for problem solving, problem solving goes more smoothly because everyone understands the process. However, it is a curse because team activity drives change in an organization and sometimes change can be bound up in processes that are too rigid.

To avoid the curse, I advocate the Vince Lombardi process. Vince Lombardi was the legendary coach of the 1960's Green Bay Packers football team, and his teams were the first to refine the power of teamwork in the game of football. Every game had a mission, victory. Every offensive play had a goal: 3 yards, 7 yards, 15 yards. Every player had a clearly defined role on every play, a pass to throw, a pattern to run, a zone to cover, an opponent to block. Yet every time a ball carrier had the ball and turned up field, Lombardi could be heard on the sidelines yelling, "run to daylight!" This is the Vince Lombardi process. It means do what it takes to move ahead. Yes, follow the process, but no, don't blindly follow the rules when you see an opportunity to advance!

Expectations make teamwork dynamic.

The fifth of the five elements of effective teamwork is expectations. Every team member must maintain an open and honest dialog with other team members about what they expect from others. This permits roles to adjust as time goes on, and it provides a vehicle for developing and sustaining the value system under which the team operates. Among the things that must have open discussion are:

- Needs: what one team member needs from others in order to perform his or her role.

- Expectations: what one team member expects another will or will not do.

- Rights: what team members are entitled to as a mater of law, organization policy, or team structure.

- Values: what team members consider important in how they do their work and how they live their lives.

The first letter of each point above creates the acronym NERV and it is commonly known as the NERV model of communication. We add a final "E" because team members have to have the NERVE to execute this type of communication if the team is to flourish. Having the nerve to execute open and honest communications creates an environment that permits the team to confront difficult issues and resolve them.

As I interviewed executives and managers for this book, I asked them to tell me, from their experience, what constituted an effective team. The answers consistently identified four characteristics.

1. Effective teams produce superb results.

2. Effective teams succeed despite encountering difficulties.

3. Members of effective teams accept responsibility for the team's output.

4. Members of effective teams take action to remove barriers and difficulties.

The open and honest communication of expectations is critical to achieving these four characteristics.

"The pursuit of truth will set you free; even if you never catch up with it."

~ Clarence Darrow (1857 - 1938) attorney

"It takes a champion. Might you be one?"

Chapter 13

Sponsors & champions

Those who choose to be in the arena.

A Fairy Tale

Throughout time men have sung songs of the great deeds of common folks succeeding in an uncommon quest. Often there is a wizard involved, but never can the wizard succeed alone. For you see, the wizard is but a catalyst, one who sets the quest in motion. In the epic tale, *The Lord of the Rings*, Gandolf the wizard could not complete the quest alone. He required the aid of a hobbit, an elf, a dwarf, and a man. And, although they required the aid of legions of supporters, they championed the cause to the end, never straying from the quest. And so it is with teamwork. The wonderous wizard has set the quest in motion. However, twin enemies, petty sorcerers and ignorance, beset the quest.

Without the aid of champions true to the cause and fixed on their destiny, the quest may fail.

Where will the champions be found?

Might you be one of them?

The Real World

Any significant change requires active champions if it is to succeed. Like any other change, for teamwork to become reality in an organization requires active championship. When Moen Incorporated first began to look seriously at the power of teamwork, Don Bireley, VP Human Resources conceived Moen University as the organization driver and recruited its director. Don clearly provided initial sponsorship while the director became the visible champion of team-based activity. I consulted with both of them from the outset and had the opportunity to facilitate executive sessions on teamwork. Following these sessions, Bruce Carbonari, then President of Moen, decided teamwork would be the foundation for the significant changes he envisioned for the organization. With Bruce's backing the path became smoother. However, the champion role was still not easy. The organization had its fair share of petty sorcerers and they were not easily defeated. But defeated they were. With Carbonari's backing and Bireley's sponsorship, Moen developed a benchmark teamwork implementation.

A similar scenario has played out in many organizations committed to using teamwork as a performance driver. The lesson is straightforward. Teamwork starts with a sponsor willing to commit his/her reputation to a successful teamwork implementation. That sponsor identifies or recruits champions in the organization whose role is to drag the effort to life and nurture it to fulfillment. Preferably early in the process, the sponsor needs to garner the support of senior executives. This is often accomplished with the help of an external consultant who can bring the experience of others to bare and debunk the many lies about teamwork. However someone internal to the organization has to lead the change and nurture teamwork. This brings us to sponsors and champions, two indispensable roles if any change is to be successful.

It all starts with sponsorship.

Sponsor: one who vouches or is responsible for a person or a thing.

Although I have discussed the role of the sponsor previously, it bears repeating. Remember our dictum, no teamwork implementation or team should ever be formed without a sponsor committed to the implementation or team's mission. Even ad hoc teams require sponsorship if they are to optimize their potential. As the one who vouches for and is responsible for the project, the sponsor, like a military general, is often above the fray. S/he is not typically a member of the team but is responsible for providing leadership. The sponsor's role includes:

- Define the scope of activity.
- Review goals and progress.
- Assist in establishing priorities.
- Serve as a role model for the team process.
- Provide access to required resources.
- Remove barriers to success.

- Provide advocacy for the team and its mission.

A strong sponsor is like having a powerful mentor. Barriers disappear, opportunities show themselves and the team tends to be amazingly successful. You'll recall from chapter 1 that we measure team success with four metrics: mission accomplishment, on time, on budget, and team learning.

Champions advance the cause.

Champion: one who fights for or defends any person or cause.

Championship differs from sponsorship in that champions work in the trenches. They do the hard work needed to bring teamwork to the fore. As a result, they get dirty and bloody. My associate, Bob Nesbit, is fond of saying "You can spot the champions. They're the ones with the arrows in their backs." What he means by this is that petty sorcerers rarely have the courage to confront the executive who sponsors change. Instead they circle the champions and take potshots wherever they can.

Yes, just as one person can be both chief cook and bottle washer, one individual can be both sponsor and champion. However the roles are different. Cooks cook and bottle washers wash bottles. Champions work the process end of teamwork. They seek out and destroy resistance to the process. They believe fervently and are willing and able to take risks to see results. The teamwork champion's role includes:

- Gain and share knowledge about teamwork and teams.

- Identify areas of support and areas of resistance in the organization.

- Do everything necessary to overcome organizational resistance.

- Insure every team has sponsorship and is properly launched.

- Insure process discipline in all teams.

Why is all this necessary?

For teamwork to be of value to the organization, it must be accepted for implementation by the organization. Unfortunately teamwork, like all good ideas, does not necessarily sell itself. A number of barriers exist in organizations, some for very legitimate reasons. Among these barriers are:

- Passions for predictability.

- No absolute authority.

- Vested interests.

- Power standoffs.

- Veils of reality.

Passions for predictability

By its very nature, teamwork involves change. Regardless of what you may have read about searching for excellence, the truth is organizations seek control and predictability. This is done to facilitate conducting business. Given a choice between a known and predictable approach, and an unknown approach that may work better, it is often easier (and safer) to go with the known.

No absolute authority.

With the maze of governmental influence, stock-holder issues, employee concerns, etc., no one individual in the organization has the ability to act without regard for other interests. As a result, any idea or change must be sold across a broad spectrum before it receives support needed to proceed.

Vested interests.

Because organizations breed petty sorcerers, there are illegitimate vested interests constantly in play. Plus, in order to ensure that significant concerns are looked out for, organizations create legitimate vested interests; i.e. marketing, purchasing, sales; that are often in conflict.

Power standoffs.

When vested interests of equal power come into conflict, a standoff occurs. In a power standoff, nothing moves. Ideas are thrown against the "molasses wall" only to be sucked into the vacuum that exists in a power standoff.

At one time the Glidden Paint Company's U.S. operations were organized into six geographic regions. While I was working with the western region, they had a purchasing manager who believed in strong centralized purchasing. His thinking was that this gave the region greater leverage with suppliers, and a resultantly lower price. One of the company's branch managers floated the idea that branch stores needed some local purchasing authority in order to take advantage of local offerings and to prevent outages of critical items. The Branch Operations Manager supported this idea. Each of these managers was looking out for their own vested interest, and each had a good business argument. Because the idea was caught between two equally powerful vested interests, it went nowhere. No one said no. No one said yes. The idea was simply absorbed by the molasses wall.

Veils of reality.

No one in the organization has a complete understanding of everything going on. We all see the "reality" of the organization from our own veiled perspective.

These and other barriers exist to some degree in all organizations. As such the success of your teamwork efforts is a function of your ability to manage these barriers. Managing the barriers to teamwork is the role of the champion. It requires one to be part salesman, part diplomat, and part warrior.

Championing involves personal risk taking. One unavoidable risk is that you will encounter resistance. Resistance takes many forms, both constructive and destructive. That is one reason Bob Nesbit says: "It is easy to spot the champions. They're the ones with the arrows in their backs!"

How to make it work.

There are many elements to the role of champion and an entire book could be devoted to exploring them. Chief among these elements are:

- Manage resistance.
- Team launch.
- Tollgate reviews.
- Celebrate success.

Let's look at each of these in more detail.

Support/Resistance Matrix

	Personal Change Low → High
Perceived Benefits High	ACTIVE SUPPORT · CONFLICT
Low	PASSIVE RESISTANCE · ACTIVE RESISTANCE

Manage resistance.

The process of managing resistance is inherent in any change effort and must be a continuous thread throughout the entire teamwork implementation. Every individual in the organization will have some perception of the benefits (or lack thereof) of the teamwork implementation. Each will also experience some degree of personal change. These two factors define the support or resistance you can expect. As pictured in the matrix to the left, people who perceive high levels of benefit and low levels of personal change can be expected to provide active support. People who perceive low levels of benefit and high levels of personal change can be expected to actively resist. Those who perceive low levels of benefit but will experience no personal change will resist you, but not actively. Those who perceive high levels of benefit but will experience high levels of personal change will be in conflict.

The support/resistance matrix defines target groups that help the champion know what needs to be done to increase overall support and reduce overall resistance.

The wise champion will begin by cementing the areas of expected active support. With this target group, s/he listens to and reinforces the benefits to be derived from the teamwork implementation and highlights the limited degree of personal change involved in deriving the benefits. The North American OEM division for Tenneco Automotive recently introduced the concept of replacing individual account representatives with sales teams. In the beginning, active support could only be expected from a small group of sales and marketing mangers. They shared the same concerns, saw the same benefits, and experienced the same market issues.

Gathering their input was critical to fleshing out the benefits of the proposal, so the concept was rather thoroughly thought through before it was ever floated to the executive team. This process provided a well thought out team proposal and insured continuing support as the concept gained acceptance.

Having buttressed the base, one then must manage the conflict group. You see, as a general rule, people really don't like change. As a result, left unattended, conflict becomes resistance. No matter how beneficial the change, the natural tendency is to resist. To overcome this, the prudent champion looks for ways to reduce the perception of personal change and continually sells the benefits so that the conflict target group recognizes the benefits they will experience are worth the pain of change. At Tenneco, existing account managers saw value in having a team approach, but their role would change significantly. As the primary contact for their accounts they would take on significant team and project management responsibility. Although their compensation would reflect this, they would experience significant personal change and saw no guarantee that the concept would work. The champion spent great effort to show how the concept would work and to reduce the perception of change so the understanding of benefits outweighed the personal pain of changing.

The next target group is the passive resistance group. This group can be difficult because of their silence. They may not like your ideas, but since they are not personally affected, they will not voice their objections. This causes two problems. One, it is very difficult to manage an objection if it is never voiced. Two, resistance from this group comes passively. They simply fail to take any action at all, none to hinder, none to help. As you might expect, the first objective in managing resistance from people in this target group is recognizing who they are. If someone will not experience personal change from the teamwork implementation and is silent on the issue, assume that person is a passive resistor. The champion needs to get this target group to verbalize perceptions of benefits or lack of benefits. Once verbalized, the task is to heighten the level of perceived benefits. Get people to understand what teamwork will do for the organization, and they will move from passive resistance to active support. At Tenneco, the controller and general manager fell into this quadrant. The controller was interested in consistent and predictable financial measures and in expense control. The G.M. was driven by the division's performance and profitability. Until these people saw the benefit of the proposal in their own terms, they could be expected to offer passive resistance. If they thought the proposal would negatively affect these interests, they would quickly become powerful active resistors.

Finally we come to the active resistors (a.k.a. petty sorcerers). The likelihood of changing the perceptions of active resistors is usually low. You can and should work to get this target group to understand the benefits of proposed changes. However you also need to minimize their ability to damage or halt the teamwork implementation. Therefore the wise champion will build support in the other three target groups before opening the Pandora's box of active resistors. At Tenneco, the engineering management group fell into this quadrant. Under the previous structure, this group had little or no customer contact and felt no customer responsibility. Theirs was the realm of invention and ideas. It was not their job to sell. The team-selling concept would use engineering resources to support customer requirements and would inextricably involve the engineering group with the customer. This significant personal change with a perceived negative benefit is the perfect formula for active resistance. Team selling champions successfully convinced many engineers of the power of customer involvement but the "pure scientists" in the group never did come around. However the champions had built sufficient support for the concept that it was implemented over the objections of the active resistors.

Throughout this discussion, I have focused on heightening the level of perceived benefits. The key to selling any change is centered on the benefits of changing. Teamwork is no different. We do teamwork implementations because they get results. The results are the primary benefit from teamwork so it is essential for the champion to focus on the successes, to celebrate them, make them known, and sell them. Even the smallest of successes help create awareness of the power of teamwork and heighten the perceived benefit of proceeding.

Team launch.

One way to help insure early successes is to be sure every team has a successful launch that gets the team up and working quickly. The sponsor or team leader should meet with each team member one-on-one before the launch session. In this meeting the sponsor or team leader should:

- Explain why the team member was selected.

- Describe the role the team member is expected to fulfill on the team.

- Solicit and respond to any questions the team member has.

- Determine what the team member needs from the sponsor.

Having had a one-on-one with each team member, a team launch meeting should be held. The purpose of this meeting is to launch the team. The outcomes are: 1) a clear understanding of the team's mission, 2) define team goals, 3) clarify each team member's roles, 4) overview the processes the team will use to do its work, and 5) exchange expectations among team members. Yes, you have seen this before. The outcomes are the five elements of effective teams.

The agenda for this meeting should include the following:

- Sponsor overviews the mission, how the mission relates to the strategic drivers of the business, and what is expected of the team.

- Team members take time to dissect the mission and internalize it. As a team, re-write the mission as they see fit for sponsor review and approval.

- Team defines the goals that must be accomplished to fulfill the mission, complete with preliminary timelines and metrics.

- Team members post their roles and solicit feedback and role clarification from team members and the team sponsor.

- Team members accept initial assignments to move goals toward completion.

- Sponsor reviews and approves the team's mission, goals, timelines, metrics, and roles.

Tollgate reviews.

Tollgate reviews help the team stay focused on results. Participants in a tollgate review include all team members, the team sponsor, and significant stakeholders in the team's mission.

These assessment and communication meetings are scheduled based on the timelines established for goal attainment by the team. The purpose of the meeting is to evaluate progress and remove barriers to success. Outcomes include:

- Update all stakeholders on milestone progress.

- Identify current and potential barriers to mission attainment.

- Define actions to deal with the barriers.

- Refocus team and stakeholders on the team's mission and goals.

"What it takes to get the innovating organization up and running is essentially the same two things all vehicles need: a person in the driver's seat and a source of power."

~ Rosabeth Moss Kanter,
    in *The Change Masters*

If you avoid the siren call of the petty sorcerer, teamwork need not be a fairy tale.

Chapter 14

Conclusions

A few final thoughts.

A Fairy Tale

In a corner of the kingdom was a simple dwelling where a young boy and his sister, lived. "Do you believe in fairy tales?" the small boy asked. "Why of course not", replied his sister. "They're only stories that adults make up to frighten small children or shelter them from reality." "Well, I believe in fairy tales," said the boy. "If fairy tales are not real then the wondrous wizard isn't real, and petty sorcerers aren't real, and neither is teamwork! I want to believe in teamwork." His sister, who was older and wiser looked at him and smiled. "Oh, those things are all very real," she said. "It's just that petty sorcerers make up fairy tales about teamwork. Like all fairy tales, they are intended to deceive us and shelter us from reality. You see they don't want us to learn the powers of teamwork."

The Real World

I started this book because I had heard too many fairy tales about teamwork. I could not understand why seemingly intelligent people worked so hard to make a simple concept so complex that it would not work. As I examined the lies (fairy tales) surrounding the teamwork concept, two things became increasingly apparent. The first is that many people, those I call petty sorcerers, are threatened by the concept. They work actively to cause team efforts to fail. This group of folks is actually not so bad. You can identify the ulterior motives behind their actions and overcome the resistance they offer. However, the second issue is more difficult.

Many well-meaning people who believe fervently in the power of teamwork have preached the lies of teamwork. In their desire to make teamwork succeed, these unwitting accomplices of the petty sorcerer make the concept too complex. Why? When they see team members in conflict they try to reduce the conflict rather than deal with the issue causing it. When they see teams struggle they provide safe havens for teamwork rather than permit people to learn from their experiences. This second group is like an overprotective parent. In the effort to prevent their child from being hurt by the world around them they fail to prepare the child to deal with the trials and tribulations of life.

Above all else, teamwork is a continuous learning experience. Consider the four measures of team success: mission accomplishment, on time, on budget, and team learning. All organization structures should be accountable for mission accomplishment, on time, and on budget. The aspect of learning as a team and as an organization helps set teamwork apart. This, combined with a strong focus on mission, creates the power of teamwork.

I recently toured Fort Sumter at the entrance to the harbor at Charlotte, South Carolina. The fort is famous for receiving the first hostile fire of the American Civil War. Looking at the cannon used to defend the fort and the harbor, one cannot help but admire the teamwork involved. When the cannon were fired, each member of the six-man cannon crew (team) had a clear role. One person sponged the barrel to clear hot embers, another loaded gunpowder and another rammed the gunpowder down the barrel before yet another person loaded the shot. One person aimed the weapon by setting the direction and elevation of the gun, and a final person lit the fuse to fire the cannon. Each individual performed his role in concert with the others in order to maximize the firing efficiency of the weapon. If one member was felled, another took up his role.

This pure example of teamwork required only five elements. Each team member understood the team's mission: defend Fort Sumter, goals: fire on and destroy targets in the cannon's field of fire, individual roles: what each team member contributed to the mission, work process: the order of events to safely and efficiently fire the cannon, and expectations: constant communication among team members. Munitions were too dear to permit live fire practice. Therefore the team got its best practice in the heat of battle. No safe haven, no shelter from reality, just the need to perform in the most ardent of circumstances.

I believe we can learn a lot from these Civil War cannon crews. We exercise our best teamwork when we keep teamwork simple. All too often we work too hard on the relationship side of the teamwork equation and forget that teams that focus on results tend to work out the relationships on their own. The more complex we make the process, the more difficult the process is to implement. We need to keep teamwork simple and process focused.

We also need to recognize that, like all methodologies, teamwork is not appropriate for every situation. Teamwork requires a level of collaborative behavior that assumes common goals and no conflicting rewards. If the goals are not in common, competition will naturally surface and may be the appropriate behavior. If the rewards are in conflict, that which gets rewarded usually gets done. The choice to compete or collaborate centers around which action leads to effective results. The conduct that is most effective is dependent upon the situation.

	Compete	**Collaborate**
Organizational Identity:	different	same
Goals:	in conflict	common
Problems:	unique	shared
Reward Structure:	win-lose	win-win

Companies offering products to the same market usually compete with one another. They have different organizational identity, market share goals that are in conflict, and market rewards where if one wins (you buy a Ford) the other must lose (Chevy lost the sale). Despite this, there are often examples of teamwork across competitive companies. These occur where the organizations share a common problem that requires combined resources to address. Automotive companies collaborate on emission controls, safety, and mileage standards. Sports teams collaborate on rules and league governance. Nations work together to resolve international disputes that impact trade or the safety of their citizens. In each of these occasions, natural competitors come together in a team effort to address common goals with common rewards.

Anytime the goals are in common. Teamwork is appropriate. After all, teamwork is nothing more than a group of people focused on a common goal. We should work to keep it that simple. Throughout this book I have advocated the five elements of effective teams: mission, goals, roles, process, and expectations as the core process for teamwork. If you must make it more complex than that, focus on the management actions I've outline throughout the chapters of this book. They facilitate the core process.

But what of the great American rugged individualist? What of the "self-made-man"? Contrary to the image of the go-it-alone rugged individualist, history shows us that from the actions of the Continental Congress in 1776 through the Industrial Revolution and the Information Age, teamwork is a fundamental American behavior. Rugged individuals we are, however it is our ability as rugged individuals to pool our individual talents and focus them on the pursuit of a common mission that makes America great. No single individual expanded our borders from coast to coast. No single individual built the Panama Canal, the Hoover Dam, or the interstate highway system. No single individual won any of our wars. No single individual took us to the moon. And no mater what Al Gore says, no single individual created the internet. All of these accomplishments required great individual efforts and great leadership, but none could have been achieved without teamwork.

Regrettably, we often find individuals in corporate America who are more focused on building empire and power than on pursuing the interests of shareholders. These individuals, when threatened by the power of teamwork, become petty sorcerers. Beware their spells and incantations! If you remember the truths that set teams free, keep mission paramount, and never let anything blind you to fulfilling it, you can and will overcome the eight lies of teamwork.

"The important thing to recognize is that it takes a team, and the team ought to get credit for the wins and the losses. Successes have many fathers, failures have none."

~ Philip Caldwell, former President and C.E.O. of Ford Motor Company

Appendix A: TEAM CHARTER

Sponsor:

Mission:

Goals	Metric	Due Date
1.		
2.		
3.		
4.		

Roles: (for each team member)

Name:

Contribution to the team	Personal Goals

Established Work Processes:

All team members have a common understanding and process knowledge in how to:

☐ Analyze situations   ☐ Coordinate

☐ Solve problems   ☐ Make decisions

☐ Plan   ☐ _____

☐ Brain storm   ☐ _____

Shared Expectations:

Needs:

Expectations:

Rights:

Values:

About the Author

Mike Wachter has served as President of Corporate Impact since January 1984. In this capacity he provides consulting and training services in: strategic planning, change leadership, organization development, leadership development, teamwork, problem solving, applied creativity, and decision making.

As a consultant/speaker he has worked with companies ranging from Fortune 500 firms such as British Petroleum, DaimlerChrysler, and Fortune Brands to small "mom & pop" businesses like Allen Pump and Colbeth Enterprises.

Prior to joining Corporate Impact, Mike held executive positions with Nordson Corporation, The Glidden Paint Company, and Diamond Shamrock Corporation. He holds a Master of Business Administration degree from Cleveland State University and a Bachelor of Arts in Sociology from Kent State University.

To order additional copies or to request leadership and teamwork support, contact:

Corporate Impact

33326 Bonnieview Drive, Suite 200
Avon Lake, OH 44012-1230

(440) 930-2477 Fax: (440) 930-2525
email: inquiry@CorpImpact.com

www.CorpImpact.com
